THE SHAKER FUR HANDBOOK

Timothy D. Rieman
& Jean M. Burks

Schiffer Publishing Ltd

4880 Lower Valley Road, Atglen, PA 19310 USA

Library of Congress Cataloging-in-Publication Data

Rieman, Timothy D.
  Shaker furniture handbook / by Timothy D. Rieman & Jean M.
Burks.
     p. cm.
  ISBN 0-7643-2001-7 (pbk.)
1. Shaker furniture. I. Burks, Jean M., 1949- II. Title.

NK2407.R545 2005
749'.088'2898—dc22

                              2004017121

Published by Schiffer Publishing Ltd.
4880 Lower Valley Road
Atglen, PA 19310
Phone: (610) 593-1777; Fax: (610) 593-2002
E-mail: Info@schifferbooks.com

Designed by Mark David Bowyer
Type set in Futura LtCn BT/Humanist521 BT

ISBN: 0-7643-2001-7
Printed in China

For the largest selection of fine reference books on this and
related subjects, please visit our web site at
www.schifferbooks.com
We are always looking for people to write books on new and
related subjects. If you have an idea for a book please contact
us at the above address.

This book may be purchased from the publisher.
Include $3.95 for shipping.
Please try your bookstore first.
You may write for a free catalog.

In Europe, Schiffer books are distributed by
Bushwood Books
6 Marksbury Ave.
Kew Gardens
Surrey TW9 4JF England
Phone: 44 (0) 20 8392-8585; Fax: 44 (0) 20 8392-9876
E-mail: info@bushwoodbooks.co.uk
Free postage in the U.K., Europe; air mail at cost.

Contents

The Background

Origins

Plate 1. Location of Shaker Communities

1. Watervliet (Niskeyuna), New York (1787-1938)
2. Mount Lebanon, New York (1787-1947)
3. Hancock, Massachusetts (1790-1960)
4. Harvard, Massachusetts (1791-1918)
5. Tyringham, Massachusetts (1792-1875)
6. Enfield, Connecticut (1792-1917)
7. Canterbury, New Hampshire (1792-1992)
8. Shirley, Massachusetts (1793-1909)
9. Enfield, New Hampshire (1793-1923)
10. Alfred, Maine (1793-1931)
11. Sabbathday Lake, Maine (1794-still active)
12. Union Village, Ohio (1805-1912)
13. Watervliet, Ohio (1806-1900)
14. Pleasant Hill, Kentucky (1806-1910)
15. South Union, Kentucky (1807-1922)
16. West Union, Indiana (1810-1827)
17. North Union, Ohio (1822-1889)
18. White Water, Ohio (1822-1916)
19. Groveland, New York (1836-1892)

Short-lived Villages

Gorham, Maine (1808-1819)
Savoy, Massachusetts (1817-1825)
Sodus Bay, New York (1826-1836)
Narcoossee, Florida (1896-c. 1920)
White Oak, Georgia (1898-1902)

LOCATION

OF

SHAKER COMMUNITIES

The United Society of Believers in Christ's Second Appearing, as the Shakers call themselves, is the most extensive, enduring, and successful utopian society, established in the eighteenth century and continuing on through the present.

They originated in Manchester, England, in the 1750s, as Quakers challenging the orthodox approaches of the established church of England. This dissident group, headed by Jane and James Wardley, was already derisively known as the Shaking Quakers or Shakers, in response to their ecstatic movements during worship. Increasingly seen as an offensive sect of troublemakers, their behavior attracted public approbation, fines, and jail sentences. Ann Lee—who became the accepted head in 1770—emerged from one period in jail after receiving a vision that the Shakers should go to America.

In 1774, Ann and her seven followers landed in New York, where they did not meet a particularly tolerant reaction from their new countrymen in the tense atmosphere leading up to the American Revolution. Their promotion of pacifism, equality of the sexes, common ownership of goods, and celibacy were maligned in this new and growing nation. The Shakers eventually settled in Niskeyuna, New York (near Albany), from where they acted as traveling missionaries, eventually establishing nineteen communities in New England, Ohio, and Kentucky by 1822. Although Mother Ann, who died in 1784, did not live to see her teachings put into practice, her able followers Father Joseph Meachem (1742-1796) and Mother Lucy Wright (1760-1821) provided stability, leadership, and organization.

Membership reached its peak during the American Civil War and is estimated at 3,000. Recruitment and retention of converts declined due to a number of factors: decrease in evangelical zeal, increase in lifestyle choice and employment opportunities due to industrialization and urbanization, and the legalization of adoption, which greatly impacted the admission of children as the next generation of members. As state provision and regulation of care and education increased, the Shaker role in these areas declined and the leadership became more elderly.

As early at 1797 one newspaper reported that the Shakers as a religious community were "dead and dying." The end of the Shakers has been reported since in various media and on numerous occasions, leading many to believe that Shaker artifacts dwell only in historic sites, museums, or in the homes of the wealthy celebrities who can afford to buy a piece of the heritage at well-publicized auction. However, more than 200 years after their arrival in America, the small but ongoing United Society of Shakers continues to live, work, and witness its faith together in Sabbathday Lake, Maine.

Mother Ann Lee predicted that the Shakers would decline almost to extinction, at which time there would be a reawakening. In a strange way, this prophecy seems to have come true. While there is only modest interest in the community itself, there is an increased interest from non-members in Shaker design and craftsmanship, spurred by the numerous television documentaries, books, and exhibits which have appeared by the twenty-first century.

For the sake of Union, Shaker communities sought to look alike as well as to think, act, and worship alike. The Shaker system of government, rules of behavior, and way of life—both external and internal—were all established at the model community founded at New Lebanon, New York, in 1787 (renamed Mount Lebanon in 1861), which quickly rose in prominence as the spiritual center of the United Society of Believers and the home of their central Ministry. Here, men and women shared equally positions of authority—both spiritual and temporal—responsibilities, and respect. This hierarchy, which was built into the leadership structure at "the Mount" as it was called, extended throughout all the Shaker villages in the following manner. Reporting to the supreme authority of the parent ministry at Mount Lebanon were communities in close geographic proximity, which constituted a Bishopric. Each bishopric was governed by a quartet of Branch Ministry leaders—two elders and two eldresses—who traveled between their Shaker sites to ensure "Union" in all things sacred and secular. Each village in turn was organized into several families of approximately fifty to one hundred and fifty people, reflecting a different level of commitment to the Shaker way of life with the Church family being the most senior. Each family was in the charge of two elders and eldresses who oversaw spiritual concerns, a staff of deacons and deaconesses who supervised domestic operations, and Trustees who managed financial transactions with the outside world in the business office.

There were several important differences between Shaker communities and their worldly neighbors. The primary distinction was size, because at their peak, Shaker communities served the needs of several hundred members living on thousands of acres. Unlike the layout of neighboring towns, where individual houses were spaced to provide privacy, Shaker structures—meetinghouse, dwelling house, and workshops—were arranged closely together according to function. From an architectural standpoint, building designs reflect the Shakers' commitment to celibacy, equality of the sexes, and communal living and consequently required dual entrances halls and stairways to accommodate the brethren and sisters separately. The Shakers' daily routine varied, depending on the time of year, the seasonal tasks at hand and the skills of the individuals. The brethren were encouraged to master two or more occupations, which not only prevented boredom but enabled the community to be less dependent on the contributions of a few key members of the society. The life of cabinetmaker Brother Isaac Newton Youngs (1793-1865) epitomizes the varied occupations pursued by one individual which are recorded in his "Biography in verse:"

"I'm overrun with work and chores
Up in the farm or within doors
Which every way I turn my eyes;
Enough to fill me with surprise.
Of tayl'ring, join'ring, farming too,
Almost all kinds that are to do,
Blacksmithing, Tinkering, mason work,
When could I find time to shirk?
Clock work, jenny work, keeping school
Enough to puzzle any fool.
An endless list of chores and notion
To keep me in perpetual motion."

The sisters were involved in a more systematic rotation of labor. They were responsible for traditional women's duties that included monthly turns in the kitchen, bakery, laundry, and housekeeping departments as well as in the dairy, spin shop, and herb house.

Unlike the Amish with whom they are often confused, the Shakers were enthusiastic agents of social as well as spiritual change and keen participants in the modernization of American society. They embraced most new technologies, welcoming laborsaving devices and improvements into their community such as water power, electricity, and indoor plumbing. They were also instruments of change and were responsible for inventions which included patent medicines, the flat broom, and an industrial washing machine, to name a few, which they shared freely with "the world" as they called non-believers.

While living apart from the surrounding towns and villages, they conducted business with society both near and far. They became successful entrepreneurs known for their honesty and engaged in agriculture, textile-related activities, mechanical arts, and woodworking. They developed a revolutionary garden seed industry, excelled in horticulture and animal husbandry, and sold sweaters, cloaks, and sewing accessories, in addition to producing woodenwares, baskets, and of course chairs and furniture for their own use as well as for sale.

Design

As they sought to create their "heaven on earth," Shaker life freed Believers from the whimsical vagaries of worldly fashion. The resulting style is an outer expression of their inner belief system and also reflects the logistical needs of a communal lifestyle where utility, simplicity, quality, order, and cleanliness are highly valued.

Shaker designs were not created in a vacuum. Since no one is born a Shaker, converts trained in worldly cabinetmaking traditions brought their taste, traditions, and technical skills with them when they joined the community. They worked from what they knew, using the ideas, forms, and patterns within their physical and intellectual reach. Thus, English taste distributed through published sources (design books), imported high style furniture, as well as more vernacular American examples from surrounding rural areas prevailed. The resulting Shaker furniture designs are not new, but rather, variations of worldly models based on community ideals, institutional needs, available materials, and the skill of the cabinetmaker. (While the forms themselves have historical antecedents, their clarity, sharpness, and institutionalization were innovative.) As they did not depend on the salability of their products in a traditional competitive marketplace, Shaker craftsmen were able to build unconventional yet highly specialized furniture to suit their communal needs. Within the community, acceptable designs were perpetuated by a traditional apprenticeship program. As a result, children adopted into the society were indentured to a skilled Shaker craftsman in order to learn various trades, such as woodworking. In this respect, the concept of appropriate design was passed on from one generation to the next.

Characterized by elegance of proportion, verticality of line, and reliance on finish rather than ornament, the Neoclassical style of furniture was becoming popular in America between the years of 1790 and 1820 and served as the basis for Shaker design. As far as specific forms are concerned, cupboards over cases of drawers, occasionally seen in worldly furniture, became commonplace in Shaker communities—both built-in and freestanding. Cases of drawers were created to provide storage for four or six Shaker brothers or sisters living in a single retiring room rather than the needs of a single individual. Counters were greatly enlarged and adapted to suit the textile and tailoring needs of the community, set on wheels, and fitted with an assortment of drawers and cupboards accessible from several sides to accommodate several believers working together. Kneehole, fall-front, slant-top, and butler's desks were created from worldly prototypes but only used by Shaker leaders for communal record keeping. Medieval trestle tables to seat large groups of people were adapted by Believers for communal dining. Three-legged or tripod stands are fitted with underhung or push-pull drawers suspended beneath the tops for the convenience of sisters' sewing activities. The production of chairs for both community use and sale to the world represents an important activity within some Shaker workshops. Throughout the years Shakers made many distinct variations, both with and without arms and rockers, based on the British prototypes of the ladderback style, an important form in the American tradition from the earliest settlements in New England. Specialized work furniture such as some of the sisters' sewing desks have no exact counterpart in worldly designs but are somewhat related to the Federal ladies' secretary popular in New England high-style centers. The decoration has been pared down and the amount of storage space with multiple drawers and work surfaces was expanded for functional tasks. Tall clocks based on worldly models ensured the punctuality that was essential to orderly communal living but the cases were drastically simplified to reflect the Shakers' religious beliefs.

However, Shaker design was also not static but evolved over time. While Queen Anne, Chippendale, and particularly early Federal styles were popular during the founding and early growth of the Eastern societies in the eighteenth century, Hepplewhite, Sheraton, and Empire designs prevailed in the West when the Ohio and Kentucky communities were established and results in a very different "look."

What makes Shaker Furniture discernable from worldly counterparts as well as recognizably unique to individual Shaker bishoprics or communities? An analysis of form draws on the concepts of balance, pattern, and scale, all of which contribute to the ultimate shape of the object. Symmetry—the distribution of equivalent forms and spaces on either side of a vertical or horizontal axis—is the most commonly used way to achieve balance. Bilateral symmetry in which the parts on either side of the axis are mirror images of each other is central to most eighteenth- and nineteenth-century worldly furniture. For example, in a chest of drawers or a cupboard the case is divided visually by a vertical center line in which each half mirrors the other. Although some Shaker furniture follows this common pattern (see **Plate 2**), other Shaker cabinetmakers regularly moved away from this rigidly held aesthetic and developed many asymmetrical forms. An important motive was to build a functional as well as aesthetically pleasing piece, causing Shaker craftsmen to create furniture to suit the community's specific needs, which often involved developing new combinations and layouts. In the counter shown in **Plate 3,** a single cupboard door is positioned opposite a much wider bank of drawers. Asymmetry was so well developed in numerous Shaker forms that is has come to be identified with Shaker design.

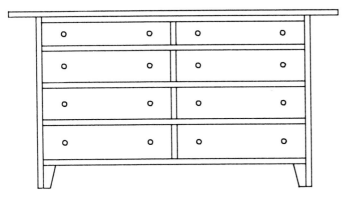

Plate 2. An example of symmetry: Counter, Mount Lebanon, New York, c. 1830.

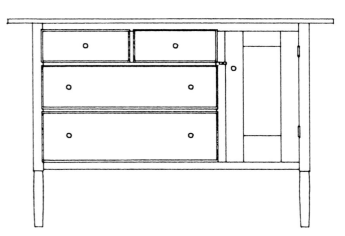

Plate 3. An example of asymmetry: Counter, attributed to Grove Wright, Hancock, Massachusetts, c. 1830.

Pattern involves the repetitive use of similar shapes, forms or spaces to create unity and organization within a design. The most common configuration is found in cases of drawers with the expected bank of graduated drawers. However, the complex counter shown in **Plate 4** utilizes two distinct drawer patterns to create an aesthetically pleasing as well as functional composition. The three drawers increase in size vertically from top to bottom, creating a rhythm typical of worldly furniture. Simultaneously, drawers decrease in width (32", 32", 22", 17", 17", and 17") horizontally across the front of the over-twelve-foot-long case. This results in an unusual but harmonious design that avoids the monotony of equal-size drawers throughout.

Plate 4. An example of pattern: Counter with drawers graduated vertically and horizontally, Mount Lebanon, New York, c. 1820.

Scale refers to the size of an object relative to its surroundings. In Shaker furniture, the dimensional relationship of a piece to its setting ranges from a diminutive 6-drawer case to the 860 built-in drawers found in a dwelling house **(Plate 5)**. Institutional requirements pushed Shaker furniture forms to a scale not seen in worldly design. Trestle tables spanning over twenty feet in length, workbench tops measuring eighteen feet long, and tailoring counters ranging from six to twelve feet in length and four feet wide all became commonplace in Shaker communities.

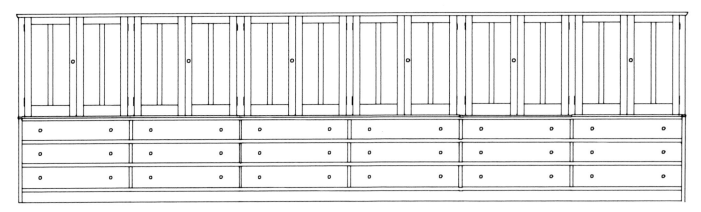

Plate 5. An example of scale: A sewing case from Hancock, Massachusetts, c. 1840, 27 inches high and 34 inches wide, compared with multiple cupboards and cases of drawers for communal storage, attic, North Family, Mount Lebanon, New York, c. 1820, approximately 7 feet high by 27 feet long.

It is easy to overlook the colorful qualities of Shaker furniture because so much of it has been stripped, refinished or repainted over the years either by the Shakers themselves or later worldly owners—due to surface wear or changing taste. Judging from extant pieces of furniture which have survived with their surfaces intact, as well as scientific analysis, color abounded in the Shaker living and work spaces. Green beds and yellow and red cupboards and cases of drawers were juxtaposed against white plastered walls. For example, the earliest pieces of Eastern Shaker furniture dating from the 1790s-1830s were coated with opaque finishes that concealed the varying woods and grain textures beneath and visually unified the piece. About 1830, however, craftsmen began to add larger amounts of plant resins to the color pigments that reduced the opacity to more of a wash. While strong colors such as red ochre, raw sienna, and chrome yellow were still used, the wood grain showed through clearly. In other pieces, particularly in the Western communities, the natural grain of the wood – such as tiger or curly maple – was used with a clear varnish finish. Toward the end of the nineteenth century, colored transparent finishes were employed.

Shaker design was not static but evolved over time. The "classical," unornamented forms of the 1820s-50s gradually gave way to a decidedly more worldly-influenced style characterized by the use of contrasting light and dark woods, bolder moldings, and glossy finishes. The Shakers were open to modernization and their interest in flexibility and change is clearly illustrated as well as stated. They embraced new modes of power for their machinery, and renovated their dwellings with commercial furniture. The 1890 edition of their publication, entitled *The Manifesto*, states, "Principles alone are regarded as a fixity; creeds, patterns, forms must in the nature of things be transitory in order to give correct expression to higher conceptions of truth and they constantly adapt modes of thought and action to the progressive principle inherent in the system" (p. 236). As a result, more liberties with furniture design began to be taken by craftsmen in several communities by the end of the nineteenth century. The range of furniture from the "plain and simple" to the "Victorian inspired" are equally valid expressions of the believers' cabinetmaking traditions and provide valuable insight into their material culture.

Mount Lebanon

The Mount Lebanon bishopric includes the Shaker communities established at New Lebanon (1787-1947)—renamed Mount Lebanon in 1861—Niskeyuna, later called Watervliet (1787-1938), and Groveland. As the first society to be officially organized, or brought into Gospel order, the largest eastern colony, and the home of the central ministry for the entire sect, Mount Lebanon assumed primary importance in both spiritual and temporal matters throughout its history.

While many of the initial converts learned their woodworking skills in the outside world and had to put aside superfluous decoration in their work as Shaker cabinetmakers, there is documentation to suggest that the training of successive generations of craftsmen occurred through long-term master-apprenticeship relationships which accounts for the continuity of Shaker design over time. Far more documented furniture produced at Mount Lebanon survives than from any other Shaker community. All major forms of Shaker work and dwelling house furniture are represented in extant examples, including cupboards, cases of drawers, counters, desks, tables, stands, and blanket boxes. Chairs were made for the community as well as for sale to the world. Classic Shaker design features are seen in the stained pine or poplar cases with plank sides and cut feet, mid-case dividing rail molding, flat-panel doors and lipped drawers with small peg-like knobs.

Figure 1. Cupboard and Case of Drawers
Mount Lebanon
c. 1840
Pine, basswood, salmon-color stain, brass latch, and steel hinges
The Mount Lebanon Shaker Collection
This piece probably represents the classic Shaker storage form—the cupboard over case of drawers. The beautifully conceived and colored unit displays several details found in Mount Lebanon casework, notably the cut foot, bull-nose cornice and the mid-case rail with the lamb's-tongue end.

Figure 2. Case of Drawers
Mount Lebanon
c. 1830
Pine, basswood, zinc yellow, raw sienna, burnt sienna pigments, varnish
The Mount Lebanon Shaker Collection
Photograph by Mark Daniels
The straight-forward design of this case of drawers is typical of Mt. Lebanon
form. The uninterrupted vertical and horizontal lines are emphasized by the
square-edged cornice, unlipped drawer fronts, and angled cut feet.

Figure 3. Case of Drawers
Mount Lebanon
c. 1840
Pine and basswood, with fruitwood knobs, and yellow wash
Shaker Museum and Library, Old Chatham, New York
Photograph by Michael Fredricks
The worldly tall chest combining half- and full-width drawers is boldly interpreted by the Shakers
with a striking yellow pigment. Measuring over six feet tall, the large size was probably designed
to accommodate the needs of two or more brothers or sisters sharing a retiring room.

Figure 4. Case of Drawers
Mount Lebanon
c. 1830
Pine with red wash and varnish
Private collection
Similar to fig. 3, these beautifully proportioned cases epitomize the classic design developed by
the Shakers over several decades at the central community at Mount Lebanon. This piece is
distinguished by its extraordinary height, systematic arrangement of drawers, and bold red wash.

Figure 5. Case of Drawers
Mount Lebanon
c. 1830
Pine, with traces of yellow paint
Hancock Shaker Village, Pittsfield, Massachusetts
This monumental piece with its dual columns of drawers closely resembles another similar
case in red paint at the Shaker Museum and Library. Built by an unidentified craftsman, both
pieces are finished with the bull-nose cornice and characteristic cut foot associated with the
Mount Lebanon community. The verticality of the design is emphasized by the use of two
identical banks of drawers and four parallel rows of turned drawer pulls.

Figure 6. Cupboard and Case of Drawers
Mount Lebanon
c. 1840
Pine and basswood, with yellow wash, brass latches, and iron hinges
Hancock Shaker Village, Pittsfield, Massachusetts
This cupboard with drawers over cupboard represents an unusual Shaker form
because of its stepback feature. However, the quarter-round cornice, plank-sided
case, unlipped drawer fronts, and cut-foot base are typical Mount Lebanon features.
Minimal decorative details are found in the beaded edge along the outside edges of the
case and the circular mounted brass latches to secure the doors on the front.

Figure 7. Cupboard and Case of Drawers
Mount Lebanon
c. 1830
Pine
Hancock Shaker Village, Pittsfield, Massachusetts
Photograph by Michael Fredricks
This pine case is particularly stark due to the absence of
base or cornice work. The door is constructed entirely of a
flat plank with battens rather than using the more traditional frame with central panel. Other unorthodox features
are seen in the size of the top drawer which is actually
larger than those below and the placement of the entire
bank of six drawers above rather than below the single
cupboard.

Figure 8. Cupboard and Case of Drawers
Mount Lebanon
c. 1840
Pine
Private collection
Although similar in overall form, this cupboard and case is very different from the previous example. Here the door is oriented above the drawers and proportionally covers most of the façade. Instead of being left plain and unadorned, the top is finished with a simple cornice.

Figure 9. Cupboard and Case of Drawers
Mount Lebanon
c. 1860
Butternut, poplar, and basswood with porcelain knobs
Printed paper labels on drawer fronts: Slippery Elm. Mug Wort. Hyssop./
Yarrow. Elder Flowers. Lobelia./ Horehound. Sweet Fern. Liver Wort.
Summer Savory. Ma[..] & Arsmart. Written in pencil in script on drawer
parts: DB [drawer bottom]: DS [drawer side]
Hancock Shaker Village, Pittsfield, Massachusetts
This is one of a pair of distinctive sill or step-back cupboards used in the
infirmary at the North Family to store medicinal herbs. Each drawer is
divided and its contents marked on the outside with paper labels. The
drawers are set high above the floor perhaps to provide additional space for
the storage of pails, boxes, or baskets beneath the case.

Figure 10. Cupboard and Case of Drawers
Mount Lebanon
c. 1870
Pine, with walnut molding, fruitwood knobs, salmon stain under varnish, brass
hinges, brass and porcelain slide latch, and chrome yellow interior
The Mount Lebanon Shaker Collection
The large cornice and contrasting applied walnut moldings are not characteristic of classic Mount Lebanon design. However, these striking worldly features
are original to this Victorian cupboard over case of drawers. The interior is
finished with a rich chrome yellow wash and the case has a salmon-colored
stain punctuated with brass and porcelain latches.

Figure 11. Cupboard and Case of Drawers
Mount Lebanon
Attributed to Austin E. Gage, house carpenter in Pittsfield, Massachusetts
1877
Ash and poplar, with porcelain knobs, cast-iron latches, and lock
The Mount Lebanon Shaker Collection
Following the devastating fires of 1875 which destroyed eight buildings in the Church Family, the
Shakers hired cabinetmakers from the world to help them replace dwelling house furniture. Appar-
ently, thirty cases like this were commissioned from Austin E. Gage, a house carpenter listed in the
1877 Pittsfield City directory. The use of ash is not common to Mt. Lebanon work, although the
classic Shaker form of cupboard over drawers was retained in designing this Victorian-era storage unit.

Figure 12. Cupboard
Mount Lebanon
c. 1830
Pine
The Mount Lebanon Shaker Collection
Photograph by Mark Daniels
Looking more like a wardrobe, this large but gracefully developed cupboard with shelves
exhibits distinctive design features. Wide stiles on each side balance the two large doors which,
because of their size, are constructed with horizontal rails and vertical stiles to separate the
eight panels. A simple quarter round molding finishes the piece on both top and bottom.

Figure 13. Cupboard
Mount Lebanon
c. 1880
Ash
Hancock Shaker Village, Pittsfield, Massachusetts
Although similar in concept to the traditional storage unit developed at Mt. Lebanon a century earlier, it is, however, constructed of ash rather than pine. This available wood was presumably chosen by the worldly craftsman who built this piece for the Shakers after the fires of 1875.

Figure 14. Fall-Front Desk
Mount Lebanon
c. 1830
Pine, with fruitwood knobs and red wash
Hancock Shaker Village, Pittsfield, Massachusetts
This small desk, measuring only two feet wide, was originally
partially built into a wall. It features the use of wide stiles surrounding the single-panel top door above narrower stiles framing the
double-panel door below. The square-edged case is softened by
cove-shaped front corners which are interrupted both above and
below the fall front door by half round rails.

Figure 15. Hanging Cupboard
Mount Lebanon
c. 1830
Pine
Private collection
Hanging cupboards are not commonplace within the
Shaker communities. This unusual example was designed
with an open shelf under the door and a characteristic
attention to detail and proportion.

Figure 16. Double Trustees' Desk
Mount Lebanon
c. 1840
Pine, with fruitwood knobs
Hancock Shaker Village, Pittsfield, Massachusetts
According to the "Millennial Laws," "All monies, book accounts, deeds, bonds, notes etc. which belong to the Church or family must be kept at the Office unless some other suitable place be provided therefore, by the proper authorities. ... The Deacons or Trustees should keep all their accounts booked down, regular and exact, and as far as possible avoid controversies with the world." The need to keep accurate business records while conducting affairs with the world required the trustees, deacons, and elders to utilize desks. This desk is associated by oral tradition with the two trustees of the Center Family. The design provides dual work and storage areas, with two cupboards concealing interior shelves, drop-front writing surfaces with shelves, pigeonholes, and small drawers above two banks of four drawers.

Figure 17. Slant-Front Desk
Mount Lebanon
c. 1840
Pine, butternut, and cherry, with fruitwood and porcelain knobs, red
wash and brass hinges, escutcheons, and locking mechanism
Private collection
The Shakers constructed slant-front as well as fall-front writing desks.
Like their worldly counterparts, the interior is fitted with pigeonholes
juxtaposed with tall ledger slots as well as a small "secret" drawer
located directly behind the top drawer in the base.

Figure 18. Table
Mount Lebanon
c. 1850
Pine with red paint
Collection Bob Hamilton
This well-proportioned
tapered leg table displays a
single drawer on the shorter
front side. The top is fitted
with a small applied rim.
Numerous styles of Shaker
furniture such as this one
were drawn directly from
worldly prototypes.

Figure 19. Counter
Benjamin Lyon (1780-1870) and Charles Weed (1831-left 1862)
1860
Written in pencil on a drawer bottom: made Feby 1860 by Benjamin Lyon and Charles Weed
Pine, cherry, and butternut with fruitwood pulls, and orange-brown stain
The Mount Lebanon Shaker Collection
According to Benjamin Lyon's journals of 1816-20, he collaborated with other joiners on a variety of
woodworking projects. However, this is the only presently known piece of furniture signed by both
Benjamin Lyon and Charles Weed. It is further documented by a reference dated March 1, 1860 in the *Farm
Journal*, 1858-1867, kept by the Second Order of the Church Family which states, "Benjamin Lyon and
Charles Weed are making a table with two rows of drawers for Hannah Train" (1783-1864). This serviceable
counter is characterized by six symmetrical unlipped drawers and a distinctive overhanging top.

Figure 20. Table
Mount Lebanon
c. 1840
Pine with metal knob
Hancock Shaker Village, Pittsfield, Massachusetts
Photograph by Michael Fredricks
This basic, tapered leg table could have been used in numerous workshops. It resembles many similar examples made outside of the Shaker communities which reveal its vernacular origins.

Figure 21. Sewing Table
Mount Lebanon
c. 1840
Cherry, pine, and poplar, with red wash
Collection Bob Hamilton
The overall delicacy of this fine sewing table was achieved by the use of a single shallow drawer, the very slender tapering legs, and the thin top. The original design was not diminished by the later Shaker addition of the second drawer below.

Figure 22. Sewing Table with Add-on
Mount Lebanon
Andrew Barrett (1836 or 1837-1917)
1830 (table), 1881 (gallery)
Written on top middle drawer: Made by Andrew Barrett Feb 1881
Cherry (table): cherry and pine, with porcelain knobs and brass pins (gallery)
Collection Bob Hamilton

This sewing table seems to be representative of the type commonly in use at Mount Lebanon soon after 1850. The design consists of either an add-on or integral gallery fitted with several narrow drawers in a variety of layouts over a base with one to three drawers on square, tapered legs.

The evolution of the sewing table probably resulted from the demographics of the Shaker communities. By the 1860s, many male members had left, and the number of new converts had declined dramatically. By the last half of the nineteenth century, a major source of income for the community had transferred to the sisters, who were extensively involved in the production of needlework.

Particularly distinctive are the small brass pins protruding from the table apron on the sides and back. Most of the sewing tables with galleries have either small brass or bone buttons around the perimeter of the base. One theory regarding their use is that they supported a fabric bag underneath the apron and between the table legs, an idea that was popular during the Federal period in America.

Figure 23. Sewing Table with Add-on
Mount Lebanon
c. 1830 (table), c. 1880 (gallery) attributed to Orren Haskins (1815-1892)
Written in pencil on underside of the upper middle drawers in the
gallery: O.N.H., June 11, 1881, Mount Lebanon, Columbia Co., N.Y.
Cherry, butternut, maple, and pine
Hancock Shaker Village, Pittsfield, Massachusetts
According to the inscription, Brother Orren Haskins refitted this 1830
two-drawer sewing table with the gallery some fifty years later for sister
Sarah Winton. Although the "Millennial Laws" of 1845 stated, "It is not
allowable for the brethren to stamp, write or mark their own names,
upon any thing which they make for the sisters," (Section XII, 5) sewing
desks made after about 1860 seem to be an exception to the rule.

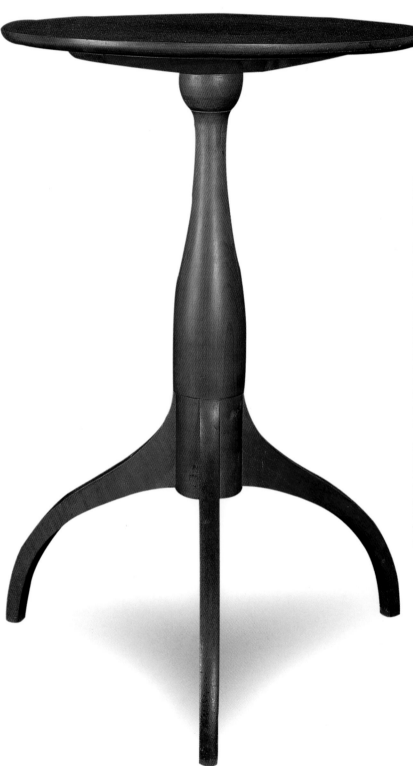

Figure 24. Tripod Stand
Mount Lebanon
Attributed to Samuel Humphrey Turner
(1775-1842)
1837
Stamped on underside of cleat: SISTER
ASENETH/ELD.S RUTH 1837
Cherry, with varnish
Private collection

The form of this spider-leg stand is typical of
the examples produced at Mount Lebanon. It
has a circular top, boldly turned pedestal with
swelled shaft, and arched tripod base.
However it is remarkable for its original finish
and documentation. The rectangular cleat
underneath, which bears the stamped
inscription, is attached with screws and has
rounded and chamfered ends to conform
with the shaped edges of the top.

Eldress Ruth probably refers to Ruth
Landon (1776-1850), who became the first
female in the lead ministry after Mother Lucy
Wright's death in 1821. Sister Aseneth Clark
(1780-1857) was her assistant. This stand was
clearly made in 1837 for these two leading
figures in the ministry at Mount Lebanon,
who as co-leaders likely shared a retiring
room in the meetinghouse.

Figure 25. Blanket Box
Mount Lebanon
c. 1840
Pine, and red wash
Hancock Shaker Village,
Pittsfield, Massachusetts
Photograph by Michael
Fredricks
The form of this six-board
box is shared by other
documented Mount Lebanon
examples. It has cut feet and
breadboard ends with integral
lip that reinforce the top and
keep it flat. The red surface
appears to be
the original finish.

Figure 26. Blanket Box
Mount Lebanon
c. 1840
Pine, with iron pulls
Shaker Museum and Library, Old
Chatham, New York
A Shaker craftsman created this
unusual blanket box complete
with interior locking mechanism.
The layout—consisting of a
shallow full-width drawer below
four half-width graduated
drawers—is, at present,
unknown on other Shaker
boxes. The cast iron Victorian
period pulls were likely applied
by the Believers to "modernize"
the piece sometime after 1880.

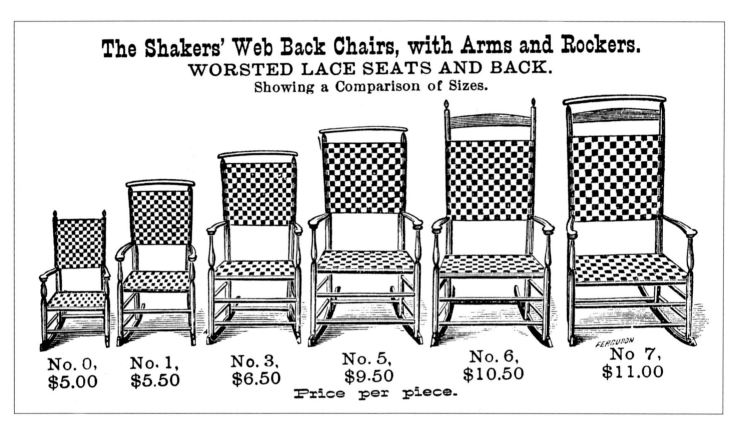

The Shakers' Web Back Chairs, with Arms and Rockers.
WORSTED LACE SEATS AND BACK.
Showing a Comparison of Sizes.

| No. 0, | No. 1, | No. 3, | No. 5, | No. 6, | No 7, |
| $5.00 | $5.50 | $6.50 | $9.50 | $10.50 | $11.00 |

Price per piece.

Figure 27. Chair Graphic
According to the Church Family account book, The Mount Lebanon Community specialized in chair making. The Shaker craftsmen here sold chairs to Believers at other communities as well as to worldly customers as early as 1789. During the nineteenth century, the East, Second, and Canaan families all had chair industries. By the 1840s the style of the Mount Lebanon chair had grown more refined and can be clearly differentiated from worldly prototypes by the following features: slimmer rear posts that taper from the seat up; pointed, oval-shaped pommels with a narrow collar; and much lighter rocker blades.

By 1850, the Second Family had assumed prominence as the leader in this business and it was during this decade that Shaker chair design reached its pinnacle. In 1863 the South Family split off from the Second Family and became the primary site of chair manufacture. As the family deacon, Brother Robert Wagan (1833-1883) skillfully managed the chair industry and was responsible for its success. Due to increased demand, the South Family built a new factory in 1872 that accommodated the development of mass-production methods, increased output, and standardization in design. Elder Henry Blinn of Canterbury visited the South Family in 1873 and described the factory and its enterprising manager in "A Journey to Kentucky":

The building erected last year, & the machinery in it has cost some $25,000. All of this was earned by this little family save $2000 which they borrowed of the Second Family. They have an engine of 15 horse power and a boiler of 20 horse power. The whole building is heated by steam. Some ten hands are employed, & it is expected that they will finish two Doz. chair per day. They are the old fashioned chairs of one hundred years ago. About two thirds are made with rockers...

One of the most singular things connected with this is, that a few years ago they made a small business in making & selling chairs, but never considered it of much importance, till it passed into the hands of the present manager. He enlarged the business and the demand has increased correspondingly. Br. Robert is enterprising. He says anything will sell that is carried into the market.

The standard factory-made chair appears about 1876 and is designed to take advantage of specialized machinery such as jigs, boring machines, and duplicating lathes. It has bolder and heavier proportions than its predecessor, with acorn-shaped pommels, prominently bent rear posts, back slats rounded on both top and bottom edges and arms shaped with two projections on the outside edge. To distinguish their products from worldly copies, the Shakers introduced a gold transfer trademark, which was applied to the chairs to guarantee authenticity.

Figure 28. Armed Rocker
Mount Lebanon
c. 1840
Figured maple
Private collection
This well proportioned side-scroll armed rocker was made for community use
for a period of thirty years with only slight variations. Characteristic details
include simply turned front posts, tapered side-scrolled arms, and back slats
with little or no graduation from top to bottom. The rocker blade style first
appeared about 1830 and continued with minor variations through 1875. This
example is somewhat finer than most due to its use of figured maple.

Figure 29. Armed Rocker
Mount Lebanon
c. 1880
Maple and cotton tape
Private collection
This size 7 rocker is typical of thousands made in the Mount Lebanon
South Family Shaker factory. The chair shows the use of steam-bent
back posts, vase-shaped front posts topped with tenon caps, and a
slightly less common cushion bar across the top of the back posts.

Figure 30. Production Chairs
Mount Lebanon
c. 1880-1910
Maple, and wool and cotton tape
Hancock Shaker Village, Pittsfield, Massachusetts
The Shakers' commitment to mass production and their careful selection of
design features created a standard form used for the following half-century.
The rungs, posts, and cushion bars of these size 0 and size 3 rockers were
turned in large quantities on production lathes.

Figure 31. Arm Chair
Mount Lebanon
c. 1930
Maple and cotton tape
Hancock Shaker Village, Pittsfield,
Massachusetts

Figure 32. Armed Rocker
Mount Lebanon
c. 1930
Maple and cotton tape
Hancock Shaker Village, Pittsfield, Massachusetts
Both this armed chair and armed rocker were made at the very end of the Shaker production during the early decades of the 20th century. At this time Sister Lillian Barlow (1876-1942) and Brother William Perkins (d. 1934) were assembling chairs from remaining stock and parts made outside of the Shaker community. Orders showed that chairs were built to customers' orders sometimes creating unusual combinations of chair styles and parts.

Watervliet and Groveland

The Mount Lebanon Bishopric includes America's first Shaker settlement, originally known by its Indian name Niskeyuna, and later called Watervliet (1787- 1938). It was the first Shaker community to produce broom corn and one of the brothers there is credited with inventing the flat broom which proved to be one of their favorite industries. They also produced clay pipes, prepared herbal medicines, and preserved vegetables hermetically sealed in tin cans—a progressive idea for its time. After the community closed in 1938, the New York State Museum in Albany actively acquired a number of pieces directly from the Shakers for its collection. It is this group of objects and their associated oral history that forms the basis of many attributions today.

Watervliet case pieces are characterized by wide, complex cornice moldings, a distinctly arched, dovetailed bracket base, and often non-graduated drawers.

Although part of the New York Bishopric, the Groveland community (1836-1892) occupied a unique role in Shaker history. It was the last village to be established, the only one to be relocated from the shores of Lake Ontario in Wayne County (in 1838) ninety miles southwest to Livingston County, and, situated midway between the eastern New York and Ohio Societies, it combined a little bit of both East and West Shaker design. In addition to agricultural products, the Groveland Shakers raised and sold cattle and lumber from their land and palm leaf bonnets which they marketed as far away as Chicago and Canada.

Early Groveland case pieces depart from common shop practice in the world or other Shaker communities in the use of either raised panels on both side of cupboard doors, or doors that extend to the side of the case without case stiles altogether. Victorian era furniture has been attributed to craftsman Emmory Brooks by Shaker sisters who knew him, whose distinctive black walnut furniture constructed of thick stock is more worldly inspired.

Figure 33. Cupboard and Case of Drawers
Watervliet
c. 1830
Pine and poplar, with original red paint
New York State Museum, Albany
This stately case piece derives much of its stature from the tall and broad applied bracket base. Raised panels punctuate the doors, a detail found only on Watervliet and Groveland cupboards. A wide projecting cornice, consisting of several different molding profiles, surmounts the top.

Figure 34. Cupboard and Case of Drawers
Possibly Watervliet
c. 1840
Pine and yellow paint with porcelain knobs
Private collection
Although certainly originating in the Northeast
Shaker communities, this colorful case piece defies
certain attribution. Its tall stance, unorthodox base
treatment, and arrangement of drawers and drawer
knobs provide a distinctive presence.

Figure 35. Bookcase
Watervliet
c. 1830
Pine and poplar or basswood, with brass escutcheons and iron hinges
and locks
Private collection
This one-piece bookcase was probably placed in or very near the
meeting room at Watervliet. The use of glass in Shaker cupboards
such as this seems to have been reserved primarily for the storage of
hymnals. The top of the case is finished with an imposing cornice
consisting of an ovolo and large cove molding suitable for a piece that
held important music or reference books.

Figure 36. Case of Drawers
Watervliet
c. 1840
Pine, with fruitwood knobs, brass
escutcheon, and lock
Private collection
The Shaker craftsman who constructed
this case did not follow conventional
practices, most readily seen in the
absence of graduated drawers. The
shaping and the bulk of both the
cornice and base are typical of designs
produced at Watervliet. It is unclear if
these characteristics point to the
practices of a shop, a small group of
workers, or a single craftsman.

Figure 37. Tall Clock
Watervliet
Benjamin Youngs, Sr. (1736-1818)
1809
Painted on front of dial: Benjamin
Youngs Water Vliet.
Written on back of face: B.Y. Fecit/
1809/B.Y. age 72/Oct. 4, 1809
Cherry and pine, with red stain and
brass movement with alarm
Private collection
Several of the tall clocks of Benjamin
Youngs, Sr. show a remarkable
development of style, both prior to his
joining the Shakers and after becoming
a Believer. As his father was a clock
maker in Connecticut, he was certainly
exposed to the more fashionable
furniture of the urban New England
areas where the Queen Anne and
Chippendale forms were in vogue.
The Shaker influence on Brother
Benjamin is found in the simplified case
and painted dial, which, aside from the
maker's name and a simple oval
surrounding it, is exclusive of typical
worldly decoration. He has consciously
omitted any brass embellishments,
veneer, inlay, or other superfluous
details so that it fits comfortably with
the Shaker community's plain, pared-
down furniture style.

Figure 38. Side Chair
Watervliet
c. 1840
Maple
Hancock Shaker Village, Pittsfield,
Massachusetts
This side chair is typical of those made
in the Watervliet community with its
strongly beveled and graduated back
slats and beautifully elongated shoul-
dered pommel. It is unfortunately not
known if Freegift Wells (1785-1871),
whose woodworking activities are well-
documented by his extensive journals,[1]
made this particular style of chair.

Figure 39. Cupboard and Case of Drawers
Groveland
c. 1840
Pine, with red wash, brass escutcheons and hinges, and iron locks
Private collection
Departing from the common shop practice in the world or other Shaker communities, some
Watervliet craftsmen built raised stiles shaped like drawer fronts on either side of their
cupboard doors. The drawers are graduated in pairs as follows: the bottom two measure a
very deep 9 1/2 inches; the next pair 7 inches; the second tier 6 inches and a single one at the
top a very narrow slender 3 1/4 inches—presumably built to suit some specific purpose.

Figure 40. Case of Drawers
Groveland
Attributed to Emmory Brooks (1807-1891)
1860-70
Walnut and pine, with varnish
New York State Museum, Albany

The overall heavy proportions and thick stock employed for rails, stiles, and drawers lend this case of drawers crafted from walnut a distinctive quality very different from the restrained simplicity of the earlier Eastern Shaker style. Sister Jennie Wells (1878-1956), a former Groveland resident, identified Brother Emmory Brooks as the maker in 1943 when she noted, "Brooks is the one I told you made so much of the Groveland black walnut furniture."

The configuration found in all of these storage units attributed to Emmory Brooks consists of two side-by-side banks of six or seven half-width drawers. This layout, whether devised for functional, structural, or purely visual reasons, is probably intentional on the part of the cabinetmaker.

Figure 41. Sewing Table
Groveland
Attributed to Emmory Brooks (1807-1891)
1860-1870
Walnut and pine, with porcelain and brass knobs
Canterbury Shaker Village, Inc., Canterbury, New Hampshire
This small, walnut sewing table with recessed gallery and square, tapered legs, is attributed to Emmory Brooks based on oral tradition. Visually, the layout of two banks of half-width drawers echoes the arrangement found in the large case pieces.

    The bold, rectilinear design of this sewing desk seems to foreshadow the furniture of the Arts and Crafts movement, which came to life in western New York within a decade of Brother Emmory's death. However, the rounded case and drawer stiles in the gallery and the notched ovolo corners of the work surface soften the overall effect of the stocky construction, while the façade gains character form the highly unusual pulls.

Figure 42. Tripod Stands
Groveland
c. 1830; curly maple with iron plate
1878; walnut with iron plate
Carved on underneath top: 1878 21 XI Presented to
Hamilton DeGraw by his friend Nicholas Tchaykovsky
Collection Fran and Herb Kramer
These two stands dating almost fifty years apart are similar
in form, although they differ in materials and numerous
design details. The inscription on the walnut stand, which
represents only part of its history, indicates it was made by
Nicholas, who with three others, were Russian guests of
the Shaker community for a year.

Hancock Bishopric

The bishopric located in western Massachusetts and Connecticut was formed by the communities of Hancock (1790-1969) and Tyringham, Massachusetts (1792-1875), and Enfield, Connecticut (1792-1917). The ministry seat was located at Hancock. As far as industries are concerned, in addition to garden seeds and woodenware, they specialized in the manufacture of collapsing table swifts for winding yarn, which they offered for sale to other Shaker societies as well as to the world.

Virtually all of the known furniture from this Bishopric was produced at either Hancock or Enfield as the Tyringham community was sold in 1876. Based on several key signed or attributed pieces, Hancock Bishopric craftsmen used a significant amount of butternut in their furniture and showed a preference for highly figured grain. Victorian era craftsmen adopted a style highly influenced by worldly taste which included a dramatic combination of light and dark woods with a clear finish and ornamental hardware consisting of commercially made cast-iron or porcelain pulls.

Figure 43. Built-in Cupboard, Case of Drawers, and Closet, Room #7, Church Family Dwelling House
Hancock
Attributed to Grove Wright (1789-1861)
1830
Pine and butternut, with fruitwood and porcelain knobs, chrome yellow paint and red ochre stain and cast-brass and forged-iron latches
Hancock Shaker Village, Pittsfield, Massachusetts
The built-in cupboards located throughout the first three floors of the Church Family dwelling provide considerable storage space for the eighty or more residents there. Constructed of butternut and pine, they were originally painted a striking red and yellow, creating a colorful room interior. The unit above with the door open reveals the original nineteenth-century chrome yellow interior. The built-in on the previous page located on the third floor reflects the Shakers' taste during the 1930-1950 period with decorative wallpaper, and linoleum covering the once-painted floor.

Figure 44. Case of Drawers
Hancock, or Enfield, Connecticut
Grove Wright (1789-1861) and Thomas
Damon (1819-1880)
1853
Written in ink on paper label glued to inside of
case: This Case of Drawers were made by/
Elder Grove and Brother Thomas and/placed
here thursday, January 13th, 1853./It was the
day our Ministry expected to/return to the City
of Peace, but were detained/on account of the
snow storm which/occured on that day.
Butternut and pine, with walnut knobs
Hancock Shaker Village, Pittsfield, Massachusetts

Monumental in size, this twelve-drawer
case designed to serve the storage needs of
several brothers or sisters is exceptionally tall
for its width. However, the configuration of
four short drawers over a bank of graduated
full-length drawers is consistent in both this
freestanding piece and in the dwelling house
built-ins. Based on the dated inscription, all of
these units were probably built by Elder Grove
Wright. He served in the Hancock Ministry
from 1816 until his death in 1861 and became
known as a woodworker producing furniture,
pails, and swifts for winding yarn.

Figure 45. Washstand and Bed
Hancock
c. 1830
Pine and maple with red paint and varnish
Hancock Shaker Village, Pittsfield, Massachusetts
This small washstand is similar to a longer washstand with two doors.
This piece is shown in the Church Family Dwelling house with a
typical Shaker bed dating from the same period. Commonly four to
six believers shared sleeping spaces in often large retiring rooms.

Figure 46. Sewing Case
Hancock
1846
Birch and butternut
Hancock Shaker Village, Pittsfield, Massachusetts
This small piece is representative of the Hancock sewing case form. Although all fifteen or so surviving pieces are petite in size, they differ in wood selection and leg shape as well as the number and arrangement of drawers. Unlike this example, some cases are fitted with a drop leaf in back or a hinged leaf in front designed to extend the work surface. The year 1846 is written on a drawer bottom, which helps to date this group of distinctive tables. The accompanying initials DW are at present unidentified.

Figure 47. Sewing Case
Hancock
c. 1840
Maple and poplar, with fruitwood
Hancock Shaker Village, Pittsfield, Massachusetts
Instead of frame and panel or apron-side construction, this petite sewing case utilizes one piece of wood for each end with a simple cutout forming the square, tapered legs. It also has a rear drop leaf with a wooden support that could be swiveled on a vertical pin. The drawer openings, which measure 2 1/2, 3, 3 5/8, and 4 5/15 inches deep, are unusually shallow.

Figure 48. Sewing Case
Hancock
c. 1840
Basswood and poplar, with brass knobs, red wash, and forged-iron crane
Hancock Shaker Village, Pittsfield, Massachusetts
This two drawer case is equipped with a rear drop leaf supported by a
forged-iron crane. The apron sides are fitted with brass knobs, perhaps
to hold various individual sewing implements or a fabric workbag. The
use of basswood as the primary material is unusual and may have been
chosen because it would not be visible under the painted surface.

Figure 49. Double Drop-Leaf Table
Hancock
c. 1830
Cherry and pine, with brass knobs and hinges
Hancock Shaker Village, Pittsfield, Massachusetts

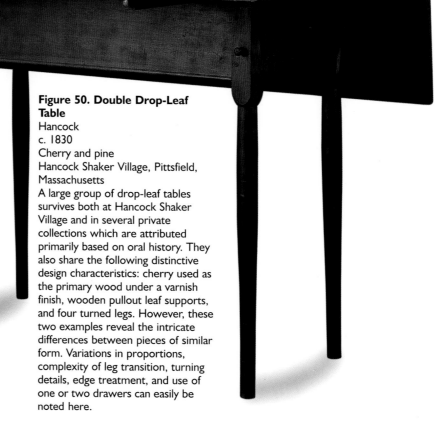

Figure 50. Double Drop-Leaf Table
Hancock
c. 1830
Cherry and pine
Hancock Shaker Village, Pittsfield, Massachusetts
A large group of drop-leaf tables survives both at Hancock Shaker Village and in several private collections which are attributed primarily based on oral history. They also share the following distinctive design characteristics: cherry used as the primary wood under a varnish finish, wooden pullout leaf supports, and four turned legs. However, these two examples reveal the intricate differences between pieces of similar form. Variations in proportions, complexity of leg transition, turning details, edge treatment, and use of one or two drawers can easily be noted here.

Figure 51. Tripod Stands
Hancock
c. 1830
Cherry and pine
Hancock Shaker Village, Pittsfield, Massachusetts
These tables both have a strong Hancock history. The one on the left features a round top with cabriole legs while the example on the right has a square-top with ovolo corners and spider legs. However, both share several characteristic construction and design features strongly associated with the Hancock Shaker community. The legs are tenoned rather than dovetailed into the pedestal base which also lacks the usual metal covering plate typical of other Shaker and worldly stands. Most notable is the shape of the turned shafts which consists of a narrow, convex ring beneath the elongated baluster-turned stem.

Figure 52. Trestle Table
Hancock
c. 1830
Maple, cherry, and birch, with varnish and iron bolts
Hancock Shaker Village, Pittsfield, Massachusetts
Photograph by Michael Fredricks
Trestle tables such as this one were commonly used in Shaker dining rooms. The absence of legs on the four corners of the table allowed for convenient use.

The base style from various communities differed considerably. However, most had an arched foot such as this one, although some used a notably flatter base. The majority were constructed from flat lumber rather than the lathe-turned vertical piece seen here.

Figure 53. Cupboard and Case of Drawers
Enfield, Connecticut
c. 1840
butternut and pine with red wash
Collection Jan and Thomas Pavolvic
This massive storage unit exhibits distinct features associated with
the Abner Allen (1776-1855) and Grove Wright (1789-1861)
school of craftsmanship found at the Enfield and Hancock
communities, respectively. The drawers are constructed with
dovetailed sides that taper in thickness from bottom to top and
the applied cornice molding is large and complex in profile.

Figure 54. Case of Drawers
Enfield, Connecticut
Abner Allen (1776-1855)
1849
Signed in pencil in script on back of drawers: May 16, 1849. Abner Allen. A.E. age 66
Butternut and pine
Private collection
Because this small case of drawers is signed and dated by the maker, it is central to the group of pieces attributed to Abner Allen. Aside from the distinctive tapered drawer construction shared by all related examples, this case is remarkable for the ogee-shaped feet and the use of butternut as the primary wood.

Figure 55. Washstand
Enfield, Connecticut
Attributed to Abner Allen (1776-1855)
c. 1830
Curly maple and pine
Private collection
The characteristic tapered drawer sides are construction features clearly associated with Brother Abner's work. The use of highly figured maple, carefully proportioned well-turned legs, and the flaring dovetailed gallery which combines the table and washstand forms represent the best of Shaker furniture design.

Figure 56. Case of Drawers
Enfield, Connecticut
Attributed to Thomas Fisher (1823-1902)
c. 1890
Written in pen in script on bottom of fifth drawer: Made in Shaker Village/THOMAS FISHER [pencil caps in different hand]/Enfield, Conn/Sister Lillian Phelps
Written in pencil in script on back of backboards: Mt. Lebanon
Written in pencil on all drawer sides and bottom and on top of corresponding rails: No 1, No 2, No 3, No 4, No 5
Chestnut, cherry, white pine, oak, and ash, with cast-iron pulls
Canterbury Shaker Village, Inc., Canterbury, New Hampshire
This five-drawer chest is one of a group of pieces attributed to Enfield, Connecticut, joiner Thomas Fisher. Although none of them bears his signature, they have been attributed to Fisher by the twentieth-century Canterbury Shakers.

Brother Thomas' distinctive style is far removed from gospel simplicity but represents an important development in Shaker design. This five-drawer case and a companion four-drawer piece clearly were designed and built as a pair. They both combine elements of the old, such as raised-panel sides, and the new, including a shaped pine backboard, varnished case surfaces, cherry top with molded edges, and commercial cast-iron pulls. Idiosyncratic features include tapered drawer sides, which are associated with other craftsmen from the Enfield and Hancock communities.

Figure 57. Pedestal Table
Enfield, Connecticut
Attributed to Thomas Fisher (1823-1902)
c. 1880
Red oak, chestnut, and cherry
Canterbury Shaker Village, Inc., Canterbury, New Hampshire
This table with octagonal top, hexagonal pedestal, and exaggerated cabriole legs terminating in modified hooves represents an innovative Shaker approach to Victorian design. Tables such as these have been attributed to Thomas Fisher on the basis of oral history and stylistic evidence. The profile of the molded top, consisting of an extended ogee, is identical to that found on both the four- and five-drawer chests (fig. 56) attributed to him by the Canterbury Shakers. The contour of many parts, including the table edge, legs, and applied facings, was clearly done with the use of a shaper.

Figure 58. Armed Rocker
Enfield, Connecticut
c. 1840
Curly maple and rush
Private collection
Rocking chairs from Enfield, Connecticut, share a basic simplicity. They are characterized by unusually tall back posts, elongated oval pommels, minimally shaped front posts with integral mushroom-shaped handholds, and high-arched graduated back slats. A noteworthy feature on most of the Enfield, Connecticut, rockers is the absence of a second tier of side stretchers, making a total of five rather than the usual seven stretchers below the seat.

Figure 59. Side Chair
Enfield, Connecticut
c. 1840
Maple and tape with green paint
Courtesy of the Art Complex Museum, Duxbury, Massachusetts
The elongated pommels over a sharply concave collar and strongly arched back
slats are distinctive to numerous known Enfield, Connecticut, chairs. However,
the most striking feature of this piece is the original dark green paint.

Harvard Bishopric

The two Shaker communities in eastern Massachusetts consisted of Harvard (1791-1818), the bishopric seat, and Shirley (1793-1909), located respectively thirty-five and forty miles west of Boston. They had a lucrative packaged seed industry, herb trade, and applesauce business which accounted for their economic success.

Surviving furniture has been documented by signed pieces as well as purchase history. A consistent design choice, which is apparent in many forms, is the preference for curved lines seen in the gracefully arched feet, rounded moldings, and drawer lips of case pieces. References in account books and journals indicate that Harvard Believers produced chairs both for home use and for sale to the world.

Figure 60. Built-In Cupboards and Cases of Drawers, Church Family Trustees' Office
Harvard
1841
Pine, with fruitwood knobs, varnish, and iron latches and locks
Private collection
The layout of this wall of built-ins includes two individual side-by-side cupboards on the right, rather than the more usual single unit found throughout the Trustees' building. The doors are separated from the drawers below by a rounded bull-nose molding. The wider central cupboard set above the chair rail, has a door following the distinctive Harvard pattern of one horizontal panel over two vertical panels.

Figure 61. Case of Drawers
Harvard
Attributed to Thomas Hammond, Jr. (1791-1880)
c. 1830
Written in pencil on the base section: Thomas Hammond this belongs to his case of draw[er]s
Pine, with ochre stain and iron bail handles
Hancock Shaker Village, Pittsfield, Massachusetts

This case of drawers is one of two known pieces with Thomas Hammonds' inscription. It exhibits several design and construction features associated with the Harvard Bishopric: the overall layout of several full-width drawers surrounded on top and bottom by half-width drawers; an underhung drawer, placed beneath the finely dovetailed separate bracket base; and the distinctive shallow curve of the foot. According to a journal reference, on August 25, 1858, "Brother Thomas returned & brot a case of draw[ers] he made at Shirley for his convenience here in the meeting house." Judging from the handles on the side of the case, this may be the same one that he built to carry back and forth between communities, a journey he often made.

Figure 62. Cupboard and Case of Drawers
Harvard
c. 1840
Pine, with yellow paint and cast-brass latches
Fruitlands Museums, Harvard, Massachusetts
Aside from its yellow paint, the most striking feature of this
storage unit is the drawer configuration. The façade is
organized into decreasing numbers of graduated drawers in
successive tiers. This unusual layout is as much a statement of
pure design on the part of the maker as it might be a response
to functional storage requirements.

Figure 63. Box
Harvard
Attributed to Ziba Winchester (1800–left 1838)
1821/1824
Painted in red on back: 1821
Written in pencil on back: [illegible]/Winchester Aged 24 1824/Ziba Winchester of Harvard
Pine, with mahogany and maple knobs, blue-green paint over orange paint, and iron hinges and lock
Hancock Shaker Village, Pittsfield, Massachusetts
This blanket box is characteristic of Harvard cabinetmakers' work with the finely shaped and
dovetailed bracket base and the underhung drawer inserted under the case. According to scientific
paint analysis, the blue-green paint is a second coat applied over the original orange surface. The two
dates suggest the piece may have been finished and painted in 1821 and the drawer added in 1824.

Figure 64. Sewing Table
Harvard
c. 1850
Pine, butternut, and basswood, with red wash
Photograph: courtesy Skinner, Inc. auctioneers and appraisers
There is little information available from written sources or documented pieces to shed light on
Harvard sewing tables. Instead of the Mount Lebanon arrangement of a recessed gallery built above
the tabletop, this Harvard table has two short drawers attached directly to the rear of the work
surface. Rather than being added on later, the drawer unit appears to be original to the piece.

Figure 65. Trestle Table
Harvard
c. 1830
Cherry
Hancock Shaker Village
Members of each Shaker family ate together in the common dining
room of their dwelling house three times a day. They favored trestle
tables because of their length, which seated a large number of brothers
or sisters and provided the comfort of unencumbered leg room.
Communal dining tables produced at Harvard are distinctively different
from their counterparts at other Shaker communities. The base is
shaped so as to produce one continuous flowing curve from the toe of
the arched base to the end of the horizontal support under the top.

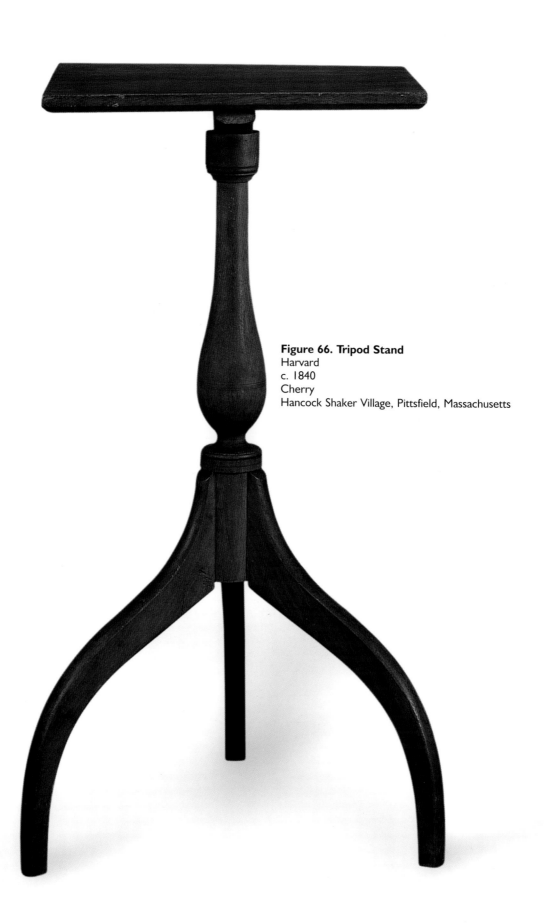

Figure 66. Tripod Stand
Harvard
c. 1840
Cherry
Hancock Shaker Village, Pittsfield, Massachusetts

New Hampshire Bishopric

The New Hampshire Bishopric consists of the Canterbury (1792-1992) and Enfield (1793-1918) Shaker communities. In addition to agricultural activities, the Canterbury Shakers developed a lucrative patent medicine industry and successfully marketed their cloaks and machine-knit sweaters to worldly customers.

Extant furniture from the New Hampshire bishopric identified by signed examples, journal records or oral history encompasses a wide variety of forms. Maple, birch, and pine were the most frequently used local woods and they were often stained or painted red or ochre color. Some freestanding cases of drawers from Canterbury exhibit plank sides with double-arched shaping known today as bootjack ends or tall ogee bracket feet derived from the Queen Anne style. Four-legged tables produced at Canterbury and Enfield are distinguished by their turned legs with a distinctive ring turning between the square and round sections. Of the at least eighty-five surviving Shaker sewing desks, most originate in the New Hampshire and Maine bishoprics. The New England Shaker interpretation of this form is more massive in design than examples produced in the Massachusetts Shaker communities, and often utilizes both the front and sides of the case for storage.

Figure 67. Built-In Cases of Drawers and Cupboards, Room 10, North Shop, Church Family
Canterbury
1841
Pine, with mustard stain and steel lock plate
Canterbury Shaker Village Inc., Canterbury, New Hampshire
The Church Family North Shop, dating from 1841, was used simultaneously as a woodshed, an herb drying area, and a dry goods storage area for the nearby community kitchen and workrooms. Although the specific purpose of Room 10 is not known, the built-in cupboards and drawers provide an example of Shaker utility cabinetwork, in comparison to the more refined dwelling house furniture. The plain cupboard doors are not embellished with a decorative molding on the interior of the frame. Drawer sides are constructed of thick, square-edged stock with plain fronts assembled with sturdy dovetails.

Figure 68. Built-in Storage Room, Attic, Church Family Dwelling House
Canterbury
1837
Pine and basswood, with yellow stain, iron hinges, and cast-iron hardware
Canterbury Shaker Village, Inc., Canterbury, New Hampshire

The ultimate Shaker built-in storage at Canterbury is the "New Attic" of the Dwelling House. Constructed in 1837 as part of a three-story addition to an earlier 1793 building, the thirty-five-foot-long room is equipped with two long under-eave storage spaces containing six walk-in closets, fourteen cupboards, and over one-hundred drawers. Metal numbers clearly mark individual units used to store off-season bedding, clothing, and crockery. All visible wood surfaces, including drawer fronts, doors, and moldings, are uniformly covered with a transparent stain, thereby revealing the grain of the pine beneath.

Figure 69. Counter
Canterbury
After 1815
Pine, with birch or maple pulls, dark blue and salmon-orange paint, and iron hinges
The Shaker Museum and Library, Old Chatham, New York
This is the earliest known documented Canterbury counter which, according to oral tradition and remaining physical evidence, was built into the south room on the third floor of the Meetinghouse, where the community leaders lived and later worked. It is painted a dark blue which matches the woodwork. In striking contrast, the interior shelves and the top were painted a salmon color. The broad asymmetrical façade, measuring almost 9 feet wide, is organized as a single cupboard, with flat-panel door, placed off center between two unequal stiles, alongside two wider banks of drawers.

Figure 70. Case of Drawers
Canterbury
c. 1840
Pine, with walnut knobs, red paint,
and brass escutcheons
Canterbury Shaker Village, Inc.,
Canterbury, New Hampshire
Photography by Bill Finney
This chest, with its unusual
grouping of shallow and deep
drawers containing paper patterns,
cloak fabric, and related materials
that were used in the community's
textile business, has never left the
site. The shallow drawers are
ideally suited to store flat pieces
and the deep drawers to hold
bonnets. Distinctive Canterbury
design features include the graceful
but sturdy ogee-shaped feet
derived from the Queen Anne
style and the double-arched skirt
on both ends of the case.

Figure 71. Counter
Canterbury
1845
Written in pencil on bottom of short drawer: Nov 1845
Pine, with porcelain pulls, wrought-iron escutcheons, slip catches, hinges, and internal locking mechanism, and brass wheels
Canterbury Shaker Village, Inc., Canterbury, New Hampshire
Measuring twelve feet long and almost four feet deep, this Canterbury work counter is the largest known Shaker example still surviving. With the addition of wheels, this counter is accessible from four sides and offers two cupboards, sixteen long drawers, and twelve short drawers to store various fabrics and related materials as well as tailoring tools. It is located in the Church Family Sisters' shop—a center for community textile activities.

Figure 72. Sewing Desk
Canterbury
Eli Kidder (1783-1867)
Written in ink on the underside of a drawer: Work Stand Made by Bro. Eli Kidder aged
77 years/Jan.1861/Moved into by M.E.H. Jan 18, 1861." MEH was probably Marcia E.
Hastings (1811-1891), based on a membership list maintained by the Canterbury
Shakers on note cards at the community and in the archives at the museum.
1861
Bird's-eye maple and pine with red stain
Shaker Museum and Library, Old Chatham, New York
Eli Kidder—the maker of this piece and another signed example located at the
Philadelphia Museum of Art—was raised as a Canterbury Shaker from childhood
where he probably learned his woodworking skills. Although the two Kidder desks are
not identical, they are closely related in design, dimensions, and materials and may
have been produced as a pair in 1861 for two different Shaker sisters. Both have
frame-and-panel construction, a bird's-eye maple work surface with slide, and drawers
on both the front and sides of the case for maximum storage.

Figure 73. Sewing Desk
Canterbury
Henry Clay Blinn (1824-1905)
c. 1870
Written on bottom of small drawer in upper gallery: These two Sewing desks were/made from Mother
Hannah's Butternut/trees, grown South of Ministries Shop. Were/cared for by her when saplings./Desks made
by Elder Henry C. Blinn. Stamped on inside of drawer faces, Arabic numerals indicating drawer placement
Butternut, bird's-eye maple, pine, and walnut, with porcelain knobs and brass latch
The Shaker Museum and Library, Old Chatham, New York
Henry Blinn served the Canterbury community as historian, author, printer, beekeeper, tailor, dentist, Church
Family leader, ministry elder, and cabinetmaker. The sewing desk—the only known signed example of Elder
Henry's furniture-making skills—follows in the tradition of Eli Kidder (see fig. 72) who was working in the
1860s. Characteristic features include the asymmetrical division of the case into drawers of unequal length, the
layout of the gallery, and the combination of dramatically figured woods. The addition of complex, contrasting
walnut moldings to the drawer faces and commercially made porcelain pulls reflects a Victorian sensibility on
the part of the maker. Mother Hannah referred to in the inscription may be Hannah Goodrich (1763-1820),
who served as first eldress of the New Hampshire ministry in 1792.

Figure 74. Blanket Box
Canterbury
c. 1830
Pine, with maple or birch pulls and gray paint
Canterbury Shaker Village, Inc., Canterbury, New Hampshire
The imposing stature of this box is created by its proportions and overall height, which is unusual for a two-drawer chest. Characteristic Canterbury construction features include the tall, broken ogee-shaped feet and small, single drawer knobs. Most important, the surface appears to retain its original finish.

Figure 75. Armed Rocker
Canterbury
c. 1830
Maple or birch, cherry with red wash, varnish and wool tape
Collection Bob Hamilton
The beautifully shaped drop-scrolled arms of this rocker differ from those used in other
Shaker bishoprics but are found in a less refined form in worldly New England chairs.
The Canterbury turners also preferred a more bulbous finial shape and broad back slats
which are generally graduated in reverse order from bottom to top. Incorporating the
form and details of the adult model, this Canterbury child size chair is indeed rare.

Figure 76. Built-In Cupboards and Cases of Drawers, Church Family Dwelling House
Enfield, New Hampshire
c. 1840
Pine
Enfield Shaker Museum, Enfield, New Hampshire
Built-ins such as these are located in many retiring rooms within the massive stone
Church Family residence, or Great Stone Dwelling. The use of built-in storage
space in the deep masonry walls of the central corridors, which entirely surround
the primary door to the retiring room, seems to be unique to the Enfield, New
Hampshire, community. According to an 1843 Shaker account,

> "Each room is accommodated with a closet which lies between the
> rooms and each room has one side of it…An offset in the partition is also
> made to accommodate a case of drawers and cupboard which is attached to
> the room, of course the room is clear, no cases of drawers, or chimney
> corners, neither woodboxes to run against."

Figure 77. Counter
Enfield, New Hampshire
c. 1840
Birch and poplar, with brass hinges and wrought-iron leaf-support mechanism
Canterbury Shaker Village, Inc., Canterbury, New Hampshire
According to an historic photograph which shows this work counter in the background, this piece clearly originated in the Enfield, New Hampshire, Shaker community. It exhibits the turned legs with distinct rings turnings between the square and round transition that is associated with New Hampshire Shaker workmanship.

Of special interest is the card table-hinged top with L-shaped wrought-iron mechanism to support the large drop leaf. With the top in the "open" position, however, the drawers are functionally unusable, because the extended tabletop swings forward over them.

Figure 78. Sewing Desk
Enfield, New Hampshire
c. 1850
Birch and pine, with hardwood or fruitwood knobs, red wash and metal escutcheon
Private collection
Photograph: courtesy John Keith Russell Antiques, Inc.
This unusual form combines the features of the small work counter and sewing
desk. The addition of the integral ten-drawer gallery and pullout slide as well as the
broader proportions of the overall piece create a larger, very different design than
most Enfield work furniture. The double-ogee-shaped gallery sides are also unique.

Figure 79. Table
Enfield, New Hampshire
c. 1830
Birch and pine with red stain and brass knob
Private collection
This form of this table is associated with Enfield as an identical example appears in a candid photograph taken in the sewing room at Enfield, New Hampshire. In addition to the typical Enfield leg with transitional ring turning, the table top has breadboard ends with rounded edges and is fastened to the apron below with screws set into screw pockets and reinforced with at least twelve redundant glue blocks. There is no top rail and the upper edge of the drawer is set flush with the underside of the tabletop.

Figure 80. Table
Enfield, New Hampshire
c. 1840
Birch and pine, with red paint
Photograph: courtesy Tom Queen
Although similar in concept to fig. 79, this example shows somewhat
less refinement in details such as the transition between the square
and round leg turning, absence of beaded edge on the drawer front
and the unusual breadboard ends on the table top.

Figure 81. Drop-Leaf Table
Enfield, New Hampshire
c. 1850
Birch and pine
Hancock Shaker Village, Inc., Pittsfield, Massachusetts
The drop-leaf table illustrated here exhibits the typical Enfield turned leg with minimal taper. However, the craftsman also added a single drawer as well as the decorative ovolo with fillet detail on the bottom edge of the apron. This table is differentiated from most worldly examples in its use of one instead of two drop leaves.

Figure 82. Bed
Enfield, New Hampshire
Attributed to Franklin Youngs (1845-1935)
c. 1880
Ash, cherry, and walnut
Canterbury Shaker Village, Inc., Canterbury, New Hampshire
In 1854, the Enfield Shakers set up a bedstead shop, which after a few years
was leased to a manufacturing company in the village of North Enfield.

This remarkable bed is closely related to one made by Shaker
craftsman Franklin Youngs for his own use, which was sold to a worldly
friend in 1923. With its applied crests and shields, it exhibits the maker's
familiarity with the Renaissance Revival style of the 1870s. On the other
hand, this bed retains remnants of its Shaker origins in the shape of the
turned Enfield leg and the frame-and-panel construction. The division of the
surface into horizontal panels of light and dark wood is an extension of the
design of the classic Shaker sewing desk of the 1860s.

Figure 83. Box
Enfield, New Hampshire
c. 1830
Pine, with hardwood pulls, red paint, iron hinges and lock, and brass escutcheon
Written in ink on manila tag tied to key: Key belongs to red Chest. Large
Collection Bob Hamilton
This is a beautifully designed and built large chest similar to a known smaller piece probably made by the same unidentified craftsman. They each have paneled lids—an unusual feature in a storage box—similarly molded edges and turned knobs, and identically shaped ogee feet.

Figure 84. Settee
Enfield, New Hampshire
c. 1840
Birch and pine, with dark brown stain and varnish
Collection Bob Hamilton
With their shaped plank seats and tapered comb at the top, Enfield's spindle-back benches reflect the influence of worldly Windsor models, produced in numerous factories in New Hampshire. However, the Shakers modified the Windsor style by omitting both the armrests and the longitudinal stretcher, resulting in an extremely delicate but fragile design. Although no extant journal corroborates the origin of the settee, oral history suggests that the Enfield Shakers built it for use in the Meetinghouse.

Maine Bishopric

The Sabbathday Lake (1792-present) and Alfred (1793-1931) communities form the Maine Bishopric. After the Civil War, the most profitable industry at Sabbathday Lake was the manufacture of oak staves for molasses hogsheads which were exported to the West Indies. According to the Metric bureau in Boston, their mill produced the first metric dry measures in the United States, beginning in 1877.

Maine Shaker furniture shares with worldly examples a simple, basic, robust character with an emphasis on colorful surfaces. Due to the continuous nature of the Sabbathday Lake community to the present, information on specific pieces has primarily been provided by oral history. Victorian era craftsmen used unusual woods such as sycamore and elm while placing an increasing emphasis on naturally figured wood with a dramatic grain such as quarter-sawn oak, bird's-eye maple, fruitwoods, and walnut. The Maine Shakers used colored pigments—staining, as well as painting their pieces colors such as bright yellow and various shades of red, often combined with a glossy finish. The influence of worldly design also emerges in startling form.

Figure 85. Cupboard and Case of Drawers
Sabbathday Lake
c. 1820
Pine, with hardwood knobs and gray-blue paint
Collection of The United Society of Shakers,
Sabbathday Lake, Maine
This early cupboard incorporates several distinctive features associated with Maine Shaker furniture. The shallow cut foot is fashioned from a horizontal rather than a vertical board, the drawers are of nailed rather than dovetailed construction, and the faces are lipped on all four sides. The top molding, which combines a square with a double ovolo, is distinctive. The case also retains its original gray-blue painted finish.

Figure 86 Blanket Box
Alfred
c. 1830
Pine, with green paint and iron hinges
Private collection
Photograph: courtesy John Keith Russell Antiques, Inc.
The shaping and construction of the bottom rail, which is rabbeted into the case
sides to form a shallow cut foot, is a feature shared with other Maine Shaker
furniture, including the cupboard and case of drawers in fig. 85. The original
striking green surface is a color not found on other Shaker furniture.

Figure 87. Counter
Alfred
Attributed to Henry Green (1844-1931)
c. 1850
Birch and pine, with red paint
Collection of The United Society of Shakers, Sabbathday Lake, Maine
This counter designed for the Shaker tailoring or seamstress trades is attributed to Henry Green by oral history. It exhibits a number of unusual features: the configuration of four over two drawers, the placement of small, single knobs on the top drawers above a pair of widely spaced larger knobs on the bottom drawers, and the proportions of the long legs in relation to the size of the case. The craftsman's decision to place color only on the drawer faces and the legs above the case rails also gives this counter an unusual appearance.

Figure 88. Writing Desk
Alfred
Attributed to Henry Green
(1844-1931)
c. 1880
Butternut and pine
Collection of The United Society of
Shakers, Sabbathday Lake, Maine

According to an 1883 Alfred account, "Brother Henry Green made three very nice writing desks, two of which were for the Ministry Sisters and [one for] Eldress Eliza Smith. They contain four larger and [inside] two small drawers a folding leaf, partings for paper and on top two shelves for books."

This desk and its companion pieces are visually a world apart from the bookcase that Brother Henry made for the library (see fig. 89), yet they were constructed during the same period. It may not be coincidental that a progressive design of this nature was specifically situated in the Trustees' Office, where worldly people visited. Placed here, it visually proved that the Shakers were not an outdated sect but actively kept abreast of contemporary fashion.

Figure 89. Bookcase
Alfred
Henry Green (1844-1931)
c. 1880
Butternut and walnut
Collection of The United Society of Shakers,
Sabbathday Lake, Maine
Henry Green brought this two-piece butternut
bookcase from Alfred to Sabbathday Lake on January
25, 1883. It is still in use today as it was originally
conceived in the Sabbathday Lake community's
library. Elder Henry is presently the best known and
probably the most prolific of all the Victorian Shaker
cabinetmakers. The case exhibits very fine traditional
joinery techniques in the dovetailed drawers and
mortise-and-tenon work. However, the use of
machinery, in particular the shaper, is evident in the
molding surrounding the rounded portions of the
glass. The decorative walnut trim contrasts with the
lighter butternut case.

Figure 90. Sewing Desk
Alfred
Attributed to Elder Joshua Bussell (1816-1900)
c. 1860
Birch and pine with red paint and varnish and porcelain and metal pulls
Collection of The United Society of Shakers, Sabbathday Lake, Maine
Photograph: courtesy John Keith Russell Antiques, Inc.
It is impossible to know what form of sewing desk was prevalent at Alfred or Sabbathday
Lake prior to mid-century. However, this example, which combines work surface and storage
space, is representative of the designs produced about 1860. Although a variety of drawer
arrangements are known to exist, the Sabbathday Lake/Alfred pieces do not appear to utilize
drawers on the side of the case as their counterparts at Canterbury. This piece is
complimented by the striking original color which has been remarkably preserved over time.

Figure 91. Fall-Front Desk
Sabbathday Lake
Delmer Wilson (1873-1961)
1895
Cherry and pine with brass pulls, hinges, chain, and lock and iron and wood casters
Collection of The United Society of Shakers, Sabbathday Lake, Maine
According to the *Sabbathday Lake Church Record and Journal*, in an entry dated December 28, 1895, "Delmer is making Sarah and Amanda a writing desk for their room in the Dwelling House." In marked deviation from earlier Shaker practice, by the end of the nineteenth century, desks were allowed in individual retiring rooms for personal use. What distinguishes this piece is the decorative vocabulary, combining chamfered vertical frame members, turned feet, applied rosettes, and a crest of startling shape. The fall-front section, a common design feature of writing furniture used at Sabbathday Lake, contains a more traditional arrangement of small drawers, pigeonholes, and ledger slots.

Figure 92. Wood Box
Sabbathday Lake
c. 1830
Pine with yellow stain
Collection of The United Society of
Shakers, Sabbathday Lake, Maine
Like much traditional furniture from
the independent Maine bishopric, or
the State of Maine itself, this basic
piece is finished in a bold coat of paint.
The kindling box consists of a carefully
dovetailed case set well above the floor
on turned legs secured through the
bottom of the box.

Figure 93. Table
Alfred
c. 1870
Birch and pine, with gray paint
Private collection
This table painted in gray exhibits the leg turning form seen most often at Alfred.
Instead of making an abrupt transition between the square and round sections, the
craftsman's lathe tool cut directly but gradually into the square post to form a full round
over an inch or two of space. Most worldly tables—and those from other Shaker
communities—took only a half-inch to complete the transition from square to round.

Figure 94. Table
Sabbathday Lake or Alfred, Maine
1840
Hardwood and pine with red paint
Canterbury Shaker Village, Inc., Canterbury, New Hampshire
The distinctive leg turning form typical of Maine bishopric tables dignifies this broad
work table. A full-width drawer and overhanging top balance the well-conceived
design. Most unique, although probably not original, is the fine decorative finish.

Figure 95. Tripod Stand
Alfred
c. 1840
Birch, with red paint
Private collection
Photograph courtesy of John Keith Russell
The exaggerated shape of the snake leg gives a flamboyant air to this
stand and sets it apart from other Shaker or worldly examples. Both
the stem and the foot are beautifully elongated, to a point that
nearly compromises the strength of the leg. The elongated stem
with graceful swell turning supports a large circular top

Figure 96. Armchair
Sabbathday Lake
Attributed to Delmer Wilson (1873-1961)
1899
Cherry and pine, with brass rod with knobs, brown velvet cushion, and casters
Collection of The United Society of Shakers, Sabbathday Lake, Maine
This one-of-a-kind example of late Shaker craftsmanship expresses in concrete form the Believers
progressive attitude and philosophical interest in change and growth. An entry in the *Sabbathday
Lake Church Record and Journal*, vol. 5, pointed out Brother Delmer's source of inspiration, the
English Arts and Crafts designer William Morris (1834-1899): "Delmer has made a nice chair for his
room. It is the form of a Morris chair. Sara [Fletcher] assists him to upolster it today."

Figure 97. Side Chair
Alfred
c. 1840
Birch and cloth tape
Collection of The United Society of Shakers, Sabbathday Lake, Maine
Most unusual in a Shaker chair of this period—and a distinguishing feature of
Alfred seating furniture—is the back post, which is bent just above the seat,
while the post above and below is straight. Other details exclusive to Alfred
work include the placement of a scribe line in the middle and largest diameter
of the rungs, showing the influence of worldly Windsor bamboo chairs.

Ohio Bishopric

The success of the Shaker way in the East, combined with the zeal to convert new members, led to a far-reaching missionary effort on the Western Frontier which resulted in the establishment of seven major communities in the early years of the nineteenth century: four in Ohio and two in Kentucky. Union Village (1805-1912) became the seat of the Western Shaker leadership and the parent of the new Ohio colonies which consisted of Watervliet (1806-1900), White Water (1822-1916), and North Union (1822-89), now Shaker Heights.

The size and longevity of Union Village, together with the documented dispersal of artifacts from the site through public auction or movement with the last remaining members to Canterbury, New Hampshire, make it somewhat easier to identify furniture produced here. Union Village cabinetmakers employed their native woods of walnut, cherry, butternut, poplar, and oak instead of the maple, birch, and pine characteristic of the Eastern communities. Rather than using a pigmented paint or stain to color the surface of the wood as was the practice in the East, the Western Shakers preferred a varnish finish to reveal the natural grain beneath. The most significant aspect of Western Shaker furniture is its close relationship to vernacular prototypes such as corner cupboards, presses, tables, sewing stands, and bedsteads.

Figure 98. Case of Drawers
Union Village
c. 1840
Curly maple and pine
Photograph: courtesy of the Art Complex Museum, Duxbury, Massachusetts
Beautifully constructed of heavily figured tiger maple, this is one of the finest Western Shaker case pieces extant. Clearly the craftsman consciously alternated the direction of the grained drawer fronts to give movement to the façade. The applied bracket raises the case well above the floor and, like many of the Union Village blanket boxes and chests of drawers, features a single drop just inside the leg itself.

Figure 99. Case of Drawers
Union Village
c. 1840
Walnut
Canterbury Shaker Village, Inc., Canterbury, New Hampshire

Figure 100. Case of Drawers
Union Village
c. 1840
Walnut
Canterbury Shaker Village, Inc., Canterbury, New Hampshire
These two Union Village cases of drawers show a clear resemblance in their wood usage
and overall style. Differences exist in the overall size and base treatment. Both were
shipped by the Ohio Shakers to New Hampshire after Union Village closed in 1912 and the
remaining members and their possessions were relocated to the Canterbury community.
The small four drawer case was used by Eldress Bertha Lindsay (1897-1990) in the kitchen
of the Trustees' building until her death.

    Here, the maker utilized a plank-sided case rather than one of frame-and-panel
construction. All the drawer faces are decorated with the characteristic beaded edge. The
chest has the characteristic cyma-curved bracket base derived from Hepplewhite styling.

Figure 101. Case of Drawers
Union Village
c. 1840
Branded on underside of top drawer support: UV
Cherry, walnut, oak, basswood, and pine, with brass pulls (not original) and varnish
Canterbury Shaker Village, Inc., Canterbury, New Hampshire
Characteristic construction features associated with Union Village include frame-and-panel-construction, a top that overhangs the case at the back edge, vertically oriented backboards, and three short drawers above full-length drawers, which are graduated in size according to worldly Empire-period fashion. The unusual base was formed with triangular pieces of wood fastened to the post and the front and side rails.

Figure 102. Corner Cupboard
Union Village
c. 1840
Walnut and poplar, with varnish
Collection the Otterbein Home Retirement Community, Lebanon, Ohio
Corner cupboards are unknown in the Eastern Shaker communities. The situation is quite
different in the Midwest, where the Ohio Shakers adapted this popular regional form for
communal use. This particular two-door cupboard is unusually small, measuring only 6 feet
high. The shallow cove cornice molding is a vernacular form, common on country furniture,
and the curved front skirt and shaped legs recall those on many cases of drawers produced at
Union Village. In overall design, it represents one of the very finest Western Shaker pieces.

Figure 103. Table
Union Village
c. 1840
Cherry
Canterbury Shaker Village, Inc., Canterbury, New Hampshire
This cherry table is characteristic of Ohio Shaker furniture in many ways. The drawer is oriented in the small end of the table, unlike most Eastern Shaker examples. The shaping of the legs consists of a square upper post with a 90-degree shoulder and a straight turned section that tapers sharply about 4 inches from the floor to form the pointed foot. The square-edged drawer face with characteristic flat knob fits flush to the rail.

Figure 104. Armed Rocker
Union Village
c. 1830
Maple, ash, and rush (not original), with cantaloupe orange paint
and rug cushion
Collection Ed Clerk
With its vibrant use of color and form, this rocker is one of the
most flamboyant pieces of Shaker seating furniture. The cantaloupe
orange paint and the exuberantly shaped arms and rocker blades
seem to be unique to Union Village. However, the craftsman
followed the Eastern Shaker traditions and used a simply contoured
back slat and turned finial without the chamfered and flattened back
in the Southern vernacular convention.

Kentucky Bishopric

The Pleasant Hill (1806-1920) and South Union (1807-1922) communities were united into a bishopric for a short period between 1868 and 1872. In addition to large-scale farming activities, they developed a thriving silkworm industry and gained an excellent reputation in cattle breeding and fruit preserving. Documented furniture from Pleasant Hill is either signed by the maker or has a strong provenance from a 1910 auction which dispersed the building contents after the community closed. As is typical of much western vernacular case furniture, each piece is solidly constructed with thick cherry or walnut stock for posts, rails, and tops. South Union furniture has been attributed through oral tradition or purchase history sold between 1920 and 1922 after the society was disbanded. Unlike Pleasant Hill or the Eastern societies, South Union furniture is much more closely related to the interior woodwork and architectural details of corresponding Shaker buildings. Furthermore, the surfaces and structural elements show a liberal use of decorative details in the form of scribe lines and applied moldings as well as shaping and turning.

Figure 105. Trestle Table
Pleasant Hill
c. 1830
Butternut
Collection of Shaker Village of Pleasant Hill, Harrodsburg, Kentucky (table); From the collection of the Harrodsburg Historical Society, Harrodsburg, Kentucky (chairs)
The broad uprights and boldly shaped, highly arched feet which support this trestle table express the spirit of Western Shaker furniture. Benches were standard dining room seating for the Pleasant Hill Believers throughout the first part of the nineteenth century. The chairs pictured here were not made by village craftsmen but purchased from the world and bear the as yet unidentified mark of M & Son painted on the bottom, perhaps to provide the brothers and sisters with more comfortable and convenient individual seating.

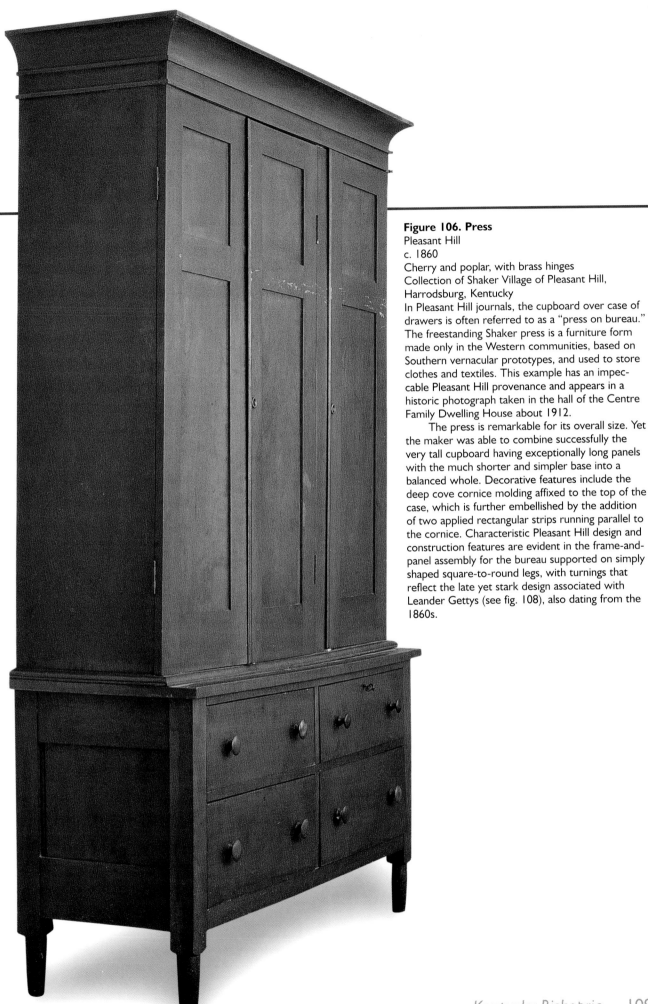

Figure 106. Press
Pleasant Hill
c. 1860
Cherry and poplar, with brass hinges
Collection of Shaker Village of Pleasant Hill,
Harrodsburg, Kentucky

In Pleasant Hill journals, the cupboard over case of
drawers is often referred to as a "press on bureau."
The freestanding Shaker press is a furniture form
made only in the Western communities, based on
Southern vernacular prototypes, and used to store
clothes and textiles. This example has an impec-
cable Pleasant Hill provenance and appears in a
historic photograph taken in the hall of the Centre
Family Dwelling House about 1912.

The press is remarkable for its overall size. Yet
the maker was able to combine successfully the
very tall cupboard having exceptionally long panels
with the much shorter and simpler base into a
balanced whole. Decorative features include the
deep cove cornice molding affixed to the top of the
case, which is further embellished by the addition
of two applied rectangular strips running parallel to
the cornice. Characteristic Pleasant Hill design and
construction features are evident in the frame-and-
panel assembly for the bureau supported on simply
shaped square-to-round legs, with turnings that
reflect the late yet stark design associated with
Leander Gettys (see fig. 108), also dating from the
1860s.

Figure 107. Case of Drawers
Pleasant Hill
c. 1840
Cherry and poplar, with varnish
Collection of Shaker Village of Pleasant Hill, Harrodsburg, Kentucky
This five-drawer case piece exhibits the big, bold proportions typical of Western Shaker furniture.
Construction details include the use of heavy frame-and-panel construction—the stiles are 2 3/4
inches wide—a square-edged top with minimal overhang, lacking embellishment, and inverted
vase-turned feet that lack a transitional shoulder between the square and turned sections.

Figure 108. Table
Pleasant Hill
Leander Gettys (1832-left 1865)
Written in black paint inside back rail: L. GETTYS, JAN. 1861
1861
Cherry and poplar, with traces of varnish
Collection of Shaker Village of Pleasant Hill, Harrodsburg, Kentucky
Only a few pieces of furniture from Pleasant Hill are known to have been signed by the maker.
This is one of two surviving tables made by Leander Gettys. According to an entry in "Temporal
Journal...Book B," possibly referring to this piece, it was produced "for the North East room 1st
story, East House by Leander Gettys" (p. 88). It is also distinguished by the absence of a transition
between the square to round sections; a wide, overhanging tabletop connected to the side and
back with numerous screws and deep pockets; and the absence of a rail above the drawer.

Figure 109. Tripod Stand and Templates
Pleasant Hill
1830-50
Cherry
Collection of Shaker Village of Pleasant Hill, Harrodsburg, Kentucky

Tripod stands were known to be placed in the halls of buildings. On April 4, 1843, according to *Temporal Journal...Book B,* "the Centre Family Dwelling House received a new candlestand in the second hall made here" (p. 7). Perhaps they served as stationary pieces to hold night lighting or functioned as easily portable stands that could be used in the family meeting room nearby.

The overall form, consisting of a pedestal on three legs, is strongly related to vernacular pieces produced during the eighteenth century in England and the colonies. Subtle details of construction create distinctions that point to a Pleasant Hill origin. Particularly noteworthy is the top, which was tapered to a thin edge on a lathe (rather than being chamfered by hand, as on many New England tables; the presence of a round "collar" (Shaker term), or disk-shaped cleat, screwed into the top from below (versus the rectangular cleat found at South Union); and the use of a metal plate secured by screws into the base of the pedestal and the legs (rather than the three staples inserted into the pedestal and legs on South Union stands).

The three templates for the leg of this stand were discovered in the eaves of the community's 1815 carpenter's shop during the restoration of the building. The *Journal of M[aurice] Thomas* records that on Wednesday, October 15, 1817, "M[icajah] Bernett and my self made some patterns" (part 2, p. 162), which could refer to templates for furniture parts such as these.

Figure 110. Bed
Pleasant Hill
c. 1830
Maple, with green paint
Collection of Shaker Village of Pleasant Hill, Harrodsburg, Kentucky
Currently located in a first floor retiring room of the Centre Family Dwelling House at Pleasant Hill, Kentucky, these narrow, single-beds with rope mattress supports are fitted for what the Shakers called wooden rollers, or wheels (now missing), so they could be moved away from a wall to facilitate cleaning underneath. However, these two Shaker beds exemplify the similarities and differences between Eastern and Western Shaker design.

Although the shaping of the legs on both examples is similar, the headboards differ significantly. The Eastern bed on the left exhibits a curved headboard and posts that consist of a cylinder over a rectangular section with transitional chamfered shoulder at either end and turned feet. In comparison, the straight Western head rail, composed of longitudinal slats, is tenoned and double-pinned to a square post that tapers on the front edge toward the turned foot.

Figure 111. Armed Rocker
Pleasant Hill
c. 1840
Hardwoods and rush seat with black paint over red
Collection of Shaker Village of Pleasant Hill, Harrodsburg, Kentucky
The unidentified craftsman displayed an unbounded exuberance in the execution of this Pleasant Hill
side chair. The strong sweep of the rockers, boldly rounded back slats, and dome-shaped handholds
applied to the nicely shaped arms provide strength to this Western Shaker rocker.

Figure 112. Side Chair
Pleasant Hill
c. 1830
Maple, hickory, oak, and splint (not original), with green paint over the original red paint
Collection of Shaker Village of Pleasant Hill, Harrodsburg, Kentucky

Figure 113. Side Chair
Pleasant Hill
c. 1830
Maple, hickory, oak, and wool tape (not original), with red paint
Collection of Shaker Village of Pleasant Hill, Harrodsburg, Kentucky
Francis Monfort (1784-1867) was a most prolific woodworker at the community and produced more chairs than any other furniture form. According to the journals, he made at least eighty-seven side chairs, fourteen armchairs, eight rocking chairs, thirty-five chairs for children, three sweating chairs for the nurses' rooms, and "one stool chair."

The proportions of the chair on the right make it one of the most delicate of all Shaker chairs. Particularly noteworthy is the unequal placement of the slats, which are 6 1/2 and 5 1/2 inches apart. The seat of the red chair is fitted with wool tape, which was woven and dyed by the Pleasant Hill Shakers as early as 1846.

Figure 114. Built-In Cupboards and Case of Drawers, Centre Family Dwelling House
South Union
1822-33
Cherry and poplar, with porcelain knobs, varnish stain, and brass hinges
The Shaker Museum at South Union, Kentucky

The brick Centre Family Dwelling House was constructed between 1822 and 1833 from local materials to house ninety covenanted members. The Georgian brick building is four stories high, with forty-two rooms and twin staircases that run top to bottom. Although the built-ins for the male and female members are not identical in layout, two-thirds of the storage units on the brothers and sisters' sides of the building are placed on the outside walls of the dwelling.

Each of the sisters' units pictured above consists of three cupboard doors over a bank of drawers, a single cupboard, and a small door (now missing) to house a chamber pot. Significant attention was given to the decorative details. The top, bottom, and sides of the built-in are surrounded by an applied complex molding and the entire unit is surmounted by a deep cornice. All drawers are adorned with porcelain knobs positioned to form a decorative oval pattern on the façade. Color also plays an important role in the overall decorative effect within the room, the ochre-stained peg rail, brick red baseboard, and clear varnish finish over the unstained cherry surfaces creating strong contrasts.

Figure 115. Press
South Union
1830-1840
Walnut, cherry, poplar, and maple, with brass knobs
The Shaker Museum at South Union, Kentucky
The South Union interpretation of this vernacular type is not only much smaller than Shaker counterparts produced at Pleasant Hill but consists of a cupboard over single-drawer base rather than full-size case of drawers. In comparison with many Pleasant Hill presses, which have a base that could be used separately, this single-drawer

unit could not have functioned independently, suggesting that the top and bottom were constructed together.

This example follows closely the architectural and decorative details found in the Centre Family Dwelling House including frame-and-panel-construction, use of the ovolo with fillet molding on the interior door frames, appearance of a single bead down the sides of the case and the presence of beaded backboards. Even the inverted baluster-turned legs and extended button feet show a remarkable resemblance to the stair post supports on each landing of the Centre Family Dwelling House.

Figure 116. Case of Drawers
South Union
c. 1830
Written in pencil on right side of top right drawer: Bought at Shaker Sale in 1919/by Chas W Jenkins for 50
00/xx/Mde in 1814 by Jesse McCoombs/member of the Shaker Colony/at South Union KY
Cherry and poplar
The Shaker Museum at South Union, Kentucky

This case of drawers has overall construction features typical of regional vernacular furniture such as frame-and-panel construction and massive proportions with heavy stock for rails, stiles, and drawer fronts. The shaping of the turned feet contributes to its weighty appearance. The case of drawers has an excellent, although perhaps exaggerated, South Union Provenance. When the community closed and the 1922 auction was held to sell the remaining furniture "made by the old time Shakers from Solid Walnut, Cherry and Oak," it is probable that the inscriptions were added to attract buyers and to enhance the sale price.

Figure 117. Case of Drawers
South Union
1852
Written in pencil in script on interior of left panel: March 1852
Walnut and poplar, with cherry knobs
The Shaker Museum at South Union, Kentucky
This case piece of frame-and-panel construction features walnut as the primary wood. It has plain drawer faces
with flat knobs original to the piece and inverted baluster-shaped feet which relate to the press shown in fig. 116.

Figure 118. Sewing Table
South Union
1860-70
Cherry and poplar, with dark varnish stain
The Shaker Museum at South Union, Kentucky

Figure 119. Sewing Table
South Union
1860-70
Cherry and poplar, with walnut knobs
The Shaker Museum at South Union, Kentucky
Western sewing tables, such as these made at South Union, present an entirely different form than their New England counterparts. The small size, splayed legs, and absence of significant drawer space or surface area suggest they were primarily used by sisters seated nearby holding handwork in their laps. This design contrasts sharply with the substantial case pieces produced in the Maine and New Hampshire communities, which provided both storage and expandable work areas for sisters seated at them (see figs. 72 and 90). Western sewing tables were based on the Federal work-table, which enjoyed popularity in East Coast urban centers from about 1785 to about 1815. The example in fig. 118, purchased from the South Union Shakers in the 1922 auction, contains a novel vertical drawer which is pulled up to access spools of thread.

Figure 120. Table
South Union
c. 1850
Walnut, with porcelain knob, brass escutcheon, and steel lock plate
The Shaker Museum at South Union, Kentucky
Not immediately recognizable as Shaker-made, this South Union table is closely related to vernacular prototypes. The massive proportions, heavy stock, and relatively elaborate turnings reflect the local cultural background of the Kentucky Believers. The gracefully sloping transitional shoulder between the short baluster leg turning and long rectangular section is repeated on the community's bedposts (see fig. 121) and the shape of the turned feet relate closely to those found on the seven drawer case piece shown in fig. 116.

Figure 121. Bed
South Union
c. 1830
Cherry
The Shaker Museum at South Union, Kentucky
The beds designed for the Believers' use reveal distinct South Union construction features. Surviving examples, such as this, are permanently pinned together, unlike beds from Eastern communities, which are easily disassembled with the removal of iron bed bolts. They consistently exhibit cyma-shaped side rails, identical head- and footboards of the same height, and distinctly turned corner posts.

Figure 122. Trestle Table
South Union
c. 1830
Walnut and ash
The Shaker Museum at South Union, Kentucky

Figure 123. Bench
South Union
c. 1830
Walnut
The Shaker Museum at South Union, Kentucky
Although trestle tables were produced in the majority of Shaker communities, those from South Union display unique design and construction features, including a top formed of numerous crosswise rather than lengthwise boards and rounded edges without breadboard ends. The substructure, which is permanently assembled and, unlike those built in the East, cannot be readily dismantled with the simple removal of several bolts and screws. Three longitudinal cleats with ogee-shaped ends are fastened to the top boards with wood screws from below.

According to a January 1, 1849, entry in *Journal B*, "Brethren on this Blessed New Years Day begin to make chairs for the dining room and so get clear of the benches."

Figure 124. Tripod Stand
South Union
c. 1840
Walnut
The Shaker Museum at South Union, Kentucky

Figure 125. Tripod Stand
South Union
1840
Written in pencil in script under top : "Meetingroom Stand"
Cherry
h 33 3/4", diameter of top 17 1/2"
The Shaker Museum at South Union, Kentucky
Surviving South Union tripod stands share common construction and design features including thick cherry or walnut tops, vase-shaped standards capped with a cylindrical turning and the liberal use of incised scribe lines as surface decoration. The underside of each leg is fitted with a 1 1/4-inch-long metal staple, which helps secure them to the vertical standard. The unusually tall stand is inscribed "Meetingroom"; according to oral tradition, it was used in the meeting room of the dwelling house as a book support or lectern for family bible readings.

Figure 126. Side Chair
South Union
c. 1820
Private collection
The typical South Union chair is distinguished by oval-shaped pommels, flattened on the top and with a noticeable ridge at the base, the whole resembling an egg "set in a cup"[2]; posts that taper sharply about one inch below the lowest stretcher to form the pointed foot; and back slats often arched on both top and lower edges. The front face of the bent back slats was shaped with a plane or draw knife, creating a somewhat rounded cross section, rather than the more typical rectangular slat.

Addresses of Shaker Villages and Museums

Canterbury Shaker Village
288 Shaker Road, Canterbury, New Hampshire 03224
Telephone: (603) 783-9511
Email: info@shakers.org
Website: http://www.shakers.org

The Enfield Shaker Museum
24 Caleb Dyer Lane, Enfield, N.H. 03748
Telephone: (603) 632-4346
Email: chosen.vale@valley.net
Website: http://www.shakermuseum.org

Hancock Shaker Village
P.O. Box 927
Rte. 20
Pittsfield, MA 01202
Telephone: (413) 443-0188 or (800) 817-1137
Email: info@hancockshakervillage.org
Website: http://www.hancockshakervillage.org

Shaker Heritage Society
1848 Shaker Meeting House
875 Watervliet Shaker Rd. Suite 2
Albany, NY 12211
Telephone: (518) 456-7890
Email: shakerwv@crisny.org
Website: http://www.crisny.org/not-for-profit/shakerwv/

The Shaker Historical Museum
16740 South Park Boulevard
Shaker Heights, Ohio 44120
Telephone: (216) 921-1201
Email: shakhist@bright.net
Website: http://www.cwru.edu/affil/shakhist/

Shaker Museum and Library
88 Shaker Museum Rd.
Old Chatham, NY 12136
Telephone: (518) 794-9100
Email: pcohen@shakermuseumandlibrary.org
Website: http://www.shakermuseumandlibrary.org/

The Shaker Museum at South Union
P.O. Box 30
South Union, Kentucky 42283
Telephone: (800) 811-8379 or (502) 542-4167
Email: shakmus@logantele.com
Website: http://www.logantele.com/~shakmus/

Shaker Village of Pleasant Hill
3501 Lexington Road. (U.S. 68)
Harrodsburg, Kentucky 40330
Telephone: 1-800-734-5611
Email: info@shakervillageky.org
Website: http://www.shakervillageky.org/home.html

Shirley Shaker Village
Shirley Historical Society
182 Center Road
PO Box 217
Shirley, MA 01464-0217
Telephone: (978) 425-9328
Email: shs1.ma.ultranet@rcn.com
Website: http://users.rcn.com/shs1.ma.ultranet/shaker.htm

The United Society of Shakers
707 Shaker Road
New Gloucester, ME 04260
Telephone: (207) 926-4597
Library email only: brooks1@shaker.lib. me.us
Office Email: usshakers@aol.com
Website: http://www.shaker.lib.me.us

Endnotes

1. Charles R. Muller and Timothy D. Rieman. *The Shaker Chair* (Schiffer Publishing, Atglen, Pennsylvania, 2003).
2. *ibid*.

For Further Reading

Grant, Jerry V. and Douglas R. Allen. *Shaker Furniture Makers.* Lebanon,
    New Hampshire: University Press of New England, 1989.
Koomler, Sharon Duane. *Shaker Style.* Courage Books, 2000.
Muller, Charles R. and Timothy D. Rieman. *The Shaker Chair.* Atglen, Penn-
    sylvania: Schiffer Publishing, 2003.
Rieman, Timothy D. *Shaker: The Art of Craftsmanship.* Alexandria, Vir-
    ginia: Art Services International, 1995.
Rieman, Timothy D. and Jean M. Burks. *The Encyclopedia of Shaker Furni-
    ture.* Atglen, Pennsylvania: Schiffer Publishing, 2003.
Stein, Stephen J. *The Shaker Experience in America.* New Haven, Con-
    necticut: Yale University Press, 1992.